T0209170

MEMORABLE
SAYINGS OF JESUS

GENE M. ADAMS

WESTBOW
PRESS®
A DIVISION OF THOMAS NELSON
& ZONDERVAN

WestBow Press books may be ordered through booksellers or by contacting:

WestBow Press
A Division of Thomas Nelson & Zondervan
1663 Liberty Drive
Bloomington, IN 47403
www.westbowpress.com
844-714-3454

ISBN: 978-1-6642-6954-5 (sc)
ISBN: 978-1-6642-6955-2 (hc)
ISBN: 978-1-6642-6956-9 (e)

Library of Congress Control Number: 2022911434

Print information available on the last page.

WestBow Press rev. date: 07/01/2022

To Sandy, my wife, not only for her contribution to this book, but also for her love and support throughout my life.

CONTENTS

INTRODUCTION

In churches throughout this land, and in lands beyond our seas, church members hold dearly in their memories given verses that have special meaning. Why does a given verse have special meaning to an individual? There are many reasons why this exists. Perhaps as a young person, an individual learned and memorized a verse such as John 3:16 (NRSV): "For God so loved the world that he gave his only son so that everyone who believes in him may not perish but have eternal life." Perhaps someone read a verse during a time of despair and grief which gave the individual support and encouragement; one possibility is Psalm 23:1 (NRSV): "The Lord is my shepherd; I shall not want." As for this writer, my favorite verse in the New Testament is John 10:10b (NRSV): "I came that they may have life and have it abundantly." As for the Old Testament, I cherish most Psalm 24:1–6, but more specifically verses 3 and 4 (ESV): "Who shall ascend the hill of the Lord? And who shall stand in his holy place? He who has clean hands and a pure heart, who does not lift up his soul to what is false and does not swear deceitfully." These verses, as written here, are what I call memorable sayings. These are verses people memorized that helped them live through the days of their life.

Therefore, I have chosen to look into the Gospels and find memorable words of Jesus which many people hold for encouragement and support. Included in this book are many of these memorable words and sayings. I am sure this collection does not include all the memorable sayings of Jesus which individuals embrace, but these in this writing include many of those sayings. With that in mind, I have titled this document *The Memorable Sayings of Jesus.*

TRANSLATIONS

In reading this book, you will discover that I did not follow only one Bible translation. I have used several translations. All of these interpretations say much the same thing; however, sometimes one translation will read more clearly than the others. It is for this reason that I chose to use the various versions, and I hope it will make this book more understandable to you as you journey through it.

Listed below are the translations that I used.

New International Version (NIV), Oxford University Press, Inc. 1982.

The Revised Standard Version (RSV), Oxford University Press, 1973.

The New Revised Standard Version (NRSV), Oxford University Press, 2007.

The Revised English Bible (REB), Oxford University Press and Cambridge *Press, 1989.*

The King James Version (KJV), 1973.

New King James Version (NKJV) Thomas Nelson Publishers, 1982.

The Anchor Bible (AB) Double Day and Co., 1981.

New International Version (NIV), Zondervan Bible Publishers, 1978.

New American Standard Bible (NASB), Zondervan Bible Publishers, 1995

SAYING 1

"Repent, for the kingdom of heaven is at hand."
—Matthew 4:17b (NKJV)

THIS IS ONE of the verses many of us learned as children in Sunday school or while at church. It was not the most popular verse, certainly not as popular as, "For God so loved the world that he gave his only son that whoever believes in him should not perish but have eternal life" (John 3:16 RSV). This passage is known by many as "the gospel in one verse." I must add that statement does not cover the entire gospel of Jesus, but it covers a large part of it. However, Matthew 4:17 was one we heard regularly.

As for Matthew 4:17, there was a problem for us as children. Since we were children, we could not understand the phrase "the kingdom of heaven." However, that did not bother us very much for we did understand the word *repent*. Stop doing the bad things which young children do and start doing good things that please your parents and please God. Well, I know that is not a thorough understanding of the Biblical word repent, but for children it was a good starting place.

Through the years, many different individuals have tried to give us a thorough understanding of the words *repent* or *repentance*. One is that to repent means to stop going in your direction, turn around, and go the other way. That means stop going toward sin and go toward Christ Jesus, or stop going in a life of sin and self-interest and go toward grace and love. Change your value system from pleasing yourself to pleasing a loving God. Stop embracing a life of materialism, greed, hate, and anger, and embrace a life of forgiveness, love of others, peace, and joy with Christ.

Perhaps one of the best understandings is given to us by Ben Witherington III when he writes that repentance means "more than just to be sorry for or to change one's mind about [sin]. It means to make a radical life change, in this case to turn away from the patterns of sin and rebellion and turn back to God and to obedience to his will."[1]

Why is repentance so important? Because God's kingdom "is at hand," and a life of peace, joy, love, and meaning is available to each one of us. God's desire for each one of us is for us to want that, or we will miss it momentarily and eternally.

---

[1] Ben Witherington III, *Matthew* (Macon, GA: Smyth & Helwys, 2006), 95.

SAYING 2

"Follow Me, and I will make you fishers of men."
—Matthew 4:19b (NKJV)

THIS IS THE beginning of Jesus calling men to be his disciples. According to Matthew, Jesus called four fishermen first: Simon (Peter), Andrew, James, and John. Why did these men respond to Jesus so readily? Could it have been that these four men were initially followers of John the Baptist? According to John 1:35–42, John the Baptist did have disciples, and some of those became followers of Jesus. Also, according to Matthew 4:12, John the Baptist had been arrested before Jesus called his disciples. Perhaps when John's disciples became aware of John's arrest, they felt lost and abandoned. They had been following John the Baptist because he had a message of knowing and following the God of Abraham, Isaac, and Jacob, much like the prophets of old. With John's arrest, they did not know where to go or what to do. In addition, they probably knew of the baptism of Jesus and the relationship of John and Jesus. Therefore, these men were ready for another prophet or teacher who knew God and would teach them how to serve God.

Jesus called these four men to follow him and be his disciples. Thus, he said to these four fishermen, "Follow me, and I will make you fishers of men." This phrase "fishers of men" seems to me to be rather strange. In the Bible, Jesus used that wording only to describe this event, as recorded in Matthew 4:19 and Mark 1:17. The Bible does not record the phrase "fishers of men" anywhere else from Genesis through Revelation. It could be that Jesus was speaking metaphorically. Jesus saw that the task of a fisherman was much like the task of a disciple. Some days fishing is good, and other days it is not. Some days a disciple will have numerous people who listen to what he says and does, and other days he will not. Thus, like a fisherman, one needs to have patience because the going can be slow. In addition, fishermen have something people really need, which is food for their hunger. Fishers of men also have something people really need, which is a message of faith and love.

SAYING 3

"Blessed are the poor in spirit,
For theirs is the kingdom of heaven."
—Matthew 5:3 (NKJV)

THIS VERSE COMES from a section in the book of Matthew referred to as "The Beatitudes." These beatitudes are statements of blessings. What do blessings entail? Well, some scholars and writers translate the word *blessing* as happy. To me, that seems to say that if we hear these sayings and enact these sayings, then we will be happy. That may be true in some accounts, but is that the essence of life? Are we trying to say that happiness is the ultimate goal and desire of our lives? Family, sports, friends, reading, money, and many other things can make me happy. But is that happiness divine? No.

Then, what is Jesus saying? I believe a blessing is far more than happiness. Being blessed is being touched by the divine hand of the Almighty. Therefore, a blessing changes our lives, alters our understanding, corrects our thinking, gives us new insight, makes us aware of God's presence in our lives, gives us purpose, gives us forgiveness leading to divine joy, and changes us in major ways. These blessings help us become more like him, and more obedient to his direction of our lives. Being blessed is a big concept, but it is God's work in our life.

A blessing may be sensing God's presence in a moment of prayer. A blessing may be sharing one's faith with another person. A blessing may be calling upon God during a period of worship. A blessing may be struggling with the scriptures to better understand what Christ is telling the reader. A blessing may be having prayer with someone in the hospital. It may be hearing "Amazing Grace" at the Cliffs of Moher in Ireland.

In this strange phrase, "poor in spirit," what is Jesus saying to us? Being poor in spirit is what we feel when we think we do not measure up to what Christ expects of us. A person who is poor in spirit is one who continually reads and studies the Scriptures, realizing that there is so much he or she does not understand. Yet the person continually strives to understand more and seek God's direction more. The life of the poor in spirit is a life of continual struggle for a better understanding of God. Too many people who claim to be Christians think they know all the answers and their task is to tell others how much they know. No! The Christian is the one who continually struggles for more understanding and a closer walk with Jesus. There is much in the Bible we cannot understand. Why? Because we are not God. We are only humans; thus, we continue to study, continue to pray, and continue to seek his face because we are the poor in spirit.

SAYING 4

"Blessed are those who mourn,
For they shall be comforted."

—Matthew 5:4 (NKJV)

IN 1965, THE singing group The Byrds recorded a popular song entitled "Turn! Turn! Turn!" or, as some people referred to it, "To Everything There is a Season." This song included the lyrics, "To everything there is a season, a time to be born and a time to die."[2] This lyric, in fact, paraphrases Ecclesiastes 3:1–2 (NRSV) of the Old Testament, which states, "For everything there is a season, and a time for every matter under heaven: a time to be born, and a time to die." This statement of Jesus in Matthew 5:4 relates to that. There is a time to be born, which usually produces joy and celebration. There is also a time to die, which produces mourning and sorrow.

There are many different incidents in life that can produce mourning and sorrow. It can occur with the loss of one's job. This job loss brings forth mourning and deep concern over how to support the family. Mourning can also come about with the destruction of one's home. What does that person do now? So many meaningful things in the house are gone. The question also arises of "Where will we stay?"

These above events are painful and create in us deep sorrow.

---

[2] The Byrds, "Turn! Turn! Turn!", 1954, *Turn! Turn! Turn!,* Columbia Records.

However, many times we experience mourning with the death of a dear friend, death of a member of the family, or death of someone important to us. The death of someone we love brings on severe mourning.

At this point, some writers begin to talk about people who mourn the sins of the world or mourn over conditions throughout the world. However, I believe Jesus was being personal. I believe Jesus was addressing the sorrow that we feel when a loved one dies. Jesus said, "Blessed are those who mourn." Such sorrow is experienced by most all people throughout the world and throughout every period in time.

How are mourning people being blessed? For one, most people who have experienced the death of a friend feel that grief. However, they also experience the slow, but painful, waning in that grief. In time, the pain usually fades away. That within itself is a blessing, but there are some people who carry their pain for years.

Second, Jesus can support and assist us in our grief. Jesus can aid us believers. We do not grieve alone. Jesus knows about death, and he sees it and feels it every day. However, he is much stronger than we are, and he cares greatly about us. Remember, Jesus said in Matthew 11:28–29 (NRSV), "Come to me, all you that are weary and are carrying heavy burdens, and I will give you rest. Take my yoke upon you and learn from me; for I am gentle and humble in heart, and you will find rest for your souls."

Third, another blessing is that we are on this earth for only a short time. When our days are over, that grief will end, and the joy of the heavenly father will overwhelm us.

Yes, those who mourn will be comforted.

SAYING 5

"You are the light of the world."

—Matthew 5:14a (NKJV)

NORMALLY IN OUR churches when we teach or preach about, or discuss light, we refer to two important concepts. One is the light mentioned in Genesis, which is the light God created. He created light so that plants, animals, and people could exist. Why do I say that? It is because after God created light, he created plants, animals, and people. According to Genesis 1:3, light was the first of God's eight acts of creation. Light was necessary for people to see, thus enabling them to engage in worship, labor, and fellowship.

The second concept is found in John 9:5b (NKJV) in Jesus's statement "I am the light of the world." Jesus says that many people at that time lived in a state of darkness—spiritual darkness. They allowed sin, doubt, unbelief, and paganism to blot out God's love, which leads to faith, redemption, grace, hope, and peace. That is what God wanted for the people of Israel. Out of his concern for them, he sent Jesus to be the light to free them from the darkness.

During the time recorded in Matthew 5:14, Jesus was calling people into a relationship of grace with him. He was telling believers that the light in him was now in them as well. Therefore, the light of Jesus was shining in them so that others would want that same light to dwell in them. Thus, the light of Jesus spread throughout the land giving people joy, forgiveness, love, and peace.

I believe the Jesus's statement, "You are the light of the world," is very clear. God's intention was that all people would experience the light of Jesus, and therefore, carry the light so that the whole world would be changed. What a revolutionary concept: change the whole world to grace, peace, hope, and joy.

The question I have is whether this has really happened. The light of Jesus still exists. People are still being changed. Nevertheless, it seems to me that the world at large is changing very little. In our country, many people claim to be followers of Jesus, but their lives show very little evidence of that. Anger, greed, hate, racism, bitterness, unfaithfulness, infidelity, violence, and a lack of concern for the poor and needy seem to be all around us.

If we Christians are the light of the world, why is it that we are not having more of an impact on our families, our towns, our states, our nation, and our world?

Oh God, please forgive us when we fail you.

SAYING 6

"Our Father who art in heaven,
Hallowed be thy name."
—Matthew 6:9b (NASB)

TO TRY TO understand this saying of Jesus, we must first begin to understand the word *hallowed*. *Hallowed* means sacred, holy, divine, set apart, and revered. This passage addresses God as sacred and set apart from us humans. It does not say that God does not value us or relate to us. It does not say that God does not love us or that God does not commune with us. The Bible is full of passages where God touched people's lives, led people, conversed with people, and provided for people. God is not so far removed from us that he has no interest in us; however, God is more than human: wiser, more powerful, more compassionate, and more loving. God is near to humans but also set apart from humans. He is holy and he is divine. Therefore, he deserves our attention, our love, our commitment, our prayers, our worship, our thoughts, our actions, and our reverence.

Now, I believe many of our churches have shifted to a position that does not recognize the holiness of God. They do not see God as being with us but beyond us. They do not see God as deserving our best. It seems to me they advocate a God who is their buddy or their pal, someone with whom they have a causal relationship. The words they use are, "God looks at the heart." That statement is true; however, God looks at more than the heart. He looks at our hands (are we helping others?); at our feet (are we walking honorably with him?); at our minds (do our thoughts give praise to him?); at our speech (are our words acceptable to him?); and at our lifestyle (is it arrogant, mean-spirited, full of greed, and missing companionship and love?). God is not a pal. He is much more than that.

God is our eternal father, our friend, our Redeemer, our creator, our teacher, our leader, and our shepherd. As such, he deserves our faith, commitment, reverence, humility, and devotion. He is much more than a buddy or a pal. He is God—separate, holy, and divine. He is our Lord and Savior.

SAYING 7

"And lead us not into temptation
but deliver us from evil."

—Matthew 6:13a (KJV)

THIS MEMORABLE SAYING of Jesus is part of a larger statement that many people refer to as the Lord's Prayer. However, I believe a more accurate title would be, the Prayer Jesus Gave His Disciples.

The wording of this saying seems a bit strange to many of us. We know Jesus would never lead anyone into temptation. Since Jesus is God in human form, we know that God is good, as stated many times in the Bible.

> Oh, give thanks to the Lord, for *He* is good! For his mercy *endures* forever. (1 Chronicles 16:34 NKJV)

> Good and upright *is* the Lord. (Psalm 25:8a NKJV)

> The Lord *is* good to all. (Psalm 145:9a NKJV)

> Oh, taste and see that the Lord *is* good! (Psalm 34:8a NKJV)

> Praise the Lord, for the Lord *is* good. (Psalm 135:3a NKJV)

The LORD *is* good, a stronghold in the day of trouble. (Nahum 1:7a NKJV)

For the Lord is good; his steadfast love endures forever. (Psalm 100:5a NKJV)

"No one is good—except God alone." (Luke 18:19b NIV)

What is Jesus saying? This is even more of a puzzle considering the words of James 1:13 (NRSV): "God cannot be tempted with evil and he himself tempts no one." Therefore, I believe what Jesus is trying to say to us is that in times of temptation, which means temptation to sin, we need the Lord to lead us. I believe these two words, "lead us," are the heart or essence of Jesus's saying.

Somewhat the same understanding is found in the second part of the saying, "deliver us from evil" or "deliver us from the evil one." I believe Jesus is saying to us that during times of temptation our prayer should be, "Lord Jesus, lead my life."

We Christians face temptations, hardships, and difficulties throughout our lives. How can we overcome much of this? I believe our help, our answers, or our aid can come from the one who truly cares about us, if we ask him to lead us.

SAYING 8-A

"You cannot serve God and mammon."
—Matthew 6:24b (NKJV)

THIS IS A very familiar saying of Jesus. To understand it better, one must see the entire statement. The statement is as follows: "No one can serve two masters; for a slave will either hate the one and love the other, or be devoted to one and despise the other. You cannot serve God and wealth" (Matthew 6:24 NRSV). The word that we are most familiar in that statement is *mammon,* which means money or wealth. Jesus says that a person cannot be a slave or a servant to God and focus on wealth or possessions at the same time.

The ancient world in which Jesus lived was somewhat like the world of today. Even though the world back then had slaves and normally we do not, still there was a large population that had no, or minimal, income, such as slaves and beggars. Today there is also a large part of our population living on minimal income. In addition, there is a much smaller part of the population that are very well-to-do. For a number of these people, wealth seems to be the reason for their existence. Jesus is addressing this group.

Having money in our society is essential to pay our bills, provide food for our families, enable our children to get an education, and cover our medical needs and other obligations that are necessary. This is understandable. This can be done without becoming enslaved or completely devoted to money or wealth. What Jesus was saying was that our devotion—our commitment—should not be to money or possessions, but to the Lord who loves us. However, for those who see wealth as the ultimate reason for their existence, there is no room for devotion to God.

In our society, we have set up the rich to be models of all for which we should strive. They are our heroes, they control our government to a large part, and they have little interest in the poor and needy. Jesus says that a person cannot be devoted to God and ignore the needs of the poor, the helpless, the sick, the lame, and the hungry. These needy people are special to our loving God.

We can only have one master and God desires to be that person.

SAYING 8-B

"You cannot serve God and mammon."

—Matthew 6:24b (NKJV)

SEVERAL YEARS AGO, while I was in my mid-twenties and was a seminary student in Louisville, Kentucky, I encountered a man I will never forget. I took my seminary classes of a morning and worked for an engineering firm on afternoons and Saturdays. The engineering firm was in midtown Louisville, where many people moved back and forth to work, to shop, to eat, and to meet other people. One afternoon as I was leaving the office, I noticed a man across the street who was begging people for money so he could get something to eat. This man was much older than I was. He wore very dirty clothes, was somewhat inebriated, and no one that I could see was willing to aid him. After watching him for a short while, I crossed the street to meet this man. He was not stable on his feet, and he smelled of alcohol. I spoke to him, told him my name, and asked him his name.

After the introductions, I asked him what he needed. He replied he needed something to eat. We then went to a small diner where I told him to get what he wanted, and I would pay for it. He ate and we talked about his home, his family, why he was in midtown Louisville, and what kind of work he had done at different times during his life. He wanted me to get him some alcohol, but I refused. I then told him that I was going to take him home and he agreed.

He lived about thirty-five miles outside of Louisville, so it took us a while to get to our destination. I walked him into his home and introduced myself to his family. They were gravely disappointed in what he had done, but they were very pleased with what I had done for him.

Did this make me a hero? No! Did this make me a model citizen? No! Then why did I do what I did? The answer is simple. I did what I did because I believed at that moment the Lord wanted me to aid this man. Why? Because this man, who was dirty, hungry, and somewhat drunk, was beloved by the Savior. He was as important to the Lord as anyone else. Thus, if Christ is our master, he has tasks for us to do. Therefore, the passage from Matthew 6:24 discusses the concept of Christ being our master.

Money is not an evil thing, but money given away to the poor and needy is a blessed thing.

SAYING 9

"Ask, and it will be given to you; seek, and you
will find; knock, and it will be opened to you.
For everyone who asks receives, and he who seeks
finds, and to him who knocks it will be opened."

—Matthew 7:7 (NKJV)

THIS PASSAGE OF ask, seek, and knock I found to be a very
difficult one for me. That was true when I was in college. I had
been a Christian since I was thirteen years of age. There was a lot
of the Bible I did not understand, but I did rest my faith on such
passages as these.

> For God so loved the world that he gave his only
> Son, that whoever believes in him should not perish
> but have eternal life. (John 3:16 NASB)

> For by grace you have been saved through faith;
> and this is not your doing, it is the gift of God—
> not because of works, lest any man should boast.
> (Ephesians 2:8–9 RSV)

> "I came that they may have life and have it
> abundantly." (John 10:10b NASB)

"Let not your hearts be troubled; believe in God, believe also in me. In my Father's house are many rooms; if it were not so, would I have told you that I go to prepare a place for you? And when I go and prepare a place for you, I will come again and take you to myself, that where I am you may be also. And you know the way where I am going." (John 14:14 RSV)

"All authority in heaven and on earth has been given to me. Go therefore and make disciples of all nations, baptizing them in the name of the Father and of the Son and of the Holy Spirit, teaching them to observe all that I have commanded you; and lo, I am with you always, to the close of the age." (Matthew 28:18b–21 RSV)

However, the test came my first year. At that time, I belonged to a Christian organization on campus, which engaged in biblical study, songs, prayers, and fellowship. We also had special speakers occasionally. As a group, we came to know one another very well. One weekend night, one of the girls had a date with someone we did not know. This couple went out of town on their date and, while returning to campus, they had a major collision. The consequence for the girl was that she had a broken neck. She was rushed to the local hospital where the hospital staff quickly attended to her. We in the organization got the news shortly after she entered the hospital. We were told that she might not make it through the night. We, as young Christians, took on the task, or privilege, of praying for her to live because we knew the verse "ask, and it will be given to you." We knew these were the words of Jesus, and she would live; if we prayed long enough and hard enough, Jesus would not let us down. He said it, so we believed it.

Later in the night, we got the word that she had died. How could that be? We prayed, we asked, and she still died. The next day, we got the information that had she lived, she would have been paralyzed from her chin down for the rest of her life. Well, that was not much comfort, but it was some help. However, the lasting problem I had, and we as a group had, was that Jesus did not spare her life.

That event did not destroy my faith, but I came away saying, "I do not understand that passage, and therefore I will ignore it." For several years following her death, I made it a point to stay away from that passage, which seemed to be very clear.

As years went by, I began to look at this passage again. First, I concluded that Jesus was always truthful, and therefore, I just did not understand. I found encouragement in writings by Theodore H. Robinson, who wrote, "Ask and some gift will be yours; seek and you will find something; knock and some door will open to you."[3] As William Barclay wrote, "Keep on asking, and it will be given you; keep on seeking, and you will find; keep on knocking, and it will be open to you. For everyone that ask receives, and he who seeks finds; and to him who knocks it will be open."[4]

Did the above statements solve my problem? No, but they did help. However, I have come to this conclusion. Asking, seeking, and knocking is our responsibility in our prayer lives. God expects and desires of us to ask, seek, and knock in our prayer lives. From these actions comes God's response—by answering, by giving, and by opening. God's response is always in loving kindness, and for our benefit. It is God's responsibility to know what answers to give and when to give them, and what gifts to give and when to give them, and what to open and when to open it. God knows what is better for us than we do.

---

[3] Theodore H. Robinson, *The Gospel of Matthew: The Moffatt New Testament Commentary* (London: Hodder and Stoughton, 1928), 63.

[4] William Barclay, *The Gospel of Matthew, Volume 1* (Philadelphia: The Westminster Press, 1958), 273.

What I have gained from this passage is to keep asking, keep seeking, and keep knocking. I look at Jesus's prayer in the garden. He asked God the Father to, "Remove this cup from me." It did not happen. The question is this: what did the Father give Jesus in return for asking? I do not know, but I do believe the Father did give Jesus something, sometime, and somewhere. It is just not for us to know.

SAYING 10

"Enter through the narrow gate; for the gate
is wide and the road is easy that leads to
destruction, and there are many who take it.
For the gate is narrow and the road is hard that
leads to life, and there are few who find it."
—Matthew 7:13–14 (NRSV)

MATTHEW 5:1–7:27 IS known as the Sermon on the Mount. I
believe a better title for this material is Sermons on the Mount. To
me, these chapters contain sermon summaries or teaching summaries
that cover numerous topics. What we have is the heart or essence of
those sermons or lessons. In Matthew 7:13–14, Jesus preaches about
life as people approach it from different ways. Jesus was not the first
biblical character to use the metaphor of two roads. In Proverbs, the
writer states in 7:1–2a (NRSV), "My child, keep my words and store
up my commandments with you; keep my commandments and live"
(road one). In 7:25–27(NRSV), he writes, "Do not let your heart
turn aside to her ways; do not stray into her paths. For many are
those she has laid low, and numerous are her victims. Her house is
the way to Sheol, going down to the chambers of death" (road two).

In Proverbs 15:24b (NRSV), a lesson is given: "For the wise,
the path of life leads upward, in order to avoid Sheol below." Thus,
we have two different roads. Also in Jeremiah 21:8, the Lord said
to Jeremiah, "See, I am setting before you the way [road] of life and

the way [road] of death." Here in Matthew 7:13–14 Jesus sets before the people two opposing ways or roads: one that leads to destruction and the other that leads to life.

In a more contemporary setting, Robert Frost gave us another two-road metaphor in his poem, "The Road Not Taken." The narrator of the poems sees "Two roads diverged in a yellow wood"— the two roads. By the end of the poem, the narrator lets us know which road he has chosen.

> I shall be telling this with a sigh
> Somewhere ages and ages hence:
> Two roads diverged in a wood, and I—
> I took the one less traveled by,
> And that has made all the difference.[5]

Where did Frost get this concept of the two ways or two roads? Did he draw this from the teachings of Jesus? Perhaps, for we know that his Scottish-born mother had a major influence on his religious development.

Now back to Jesus and his two roads. The first road, Jesus says, leads to destruction. By the word *destruction*, he means that it leads to a life that is without spiritual meaning or purpose. Such a life is a life lived with no faith in the God who loves us, no meaningful direction, no hope for the future, no peace within, and no grace. By the second road, he means a road that leads to life, as he stated in John 10:10. By life, he means faith, grace, hope, and assurance of life eternal. According to Jesus, few people walk the road to life and most people walk the road to death and destruction.

---

[5] Robert Frost, "The Road Not Taken," Poetry Foundation, accessed February 23, 2022, https://www.poetryfoundation.org/poems/44272/the-road-not-taken

SAYING 11

"Not everyone who says to me, 'Lord, Lord,'
shall enter the kingdom of heaven, but he who
does the will of my Father who is in heaven."

—Matthew 7:21 (RSV)

IN ANCIENT JUDAISM, words—spoken words—had meaning and could effect change. An example of this is in Genesis 1:3 (RSV), which reads, "And God said, 'Let there be light;' and there was light." God spoke the words and light appeared. Also in Genesis 1:26a (RSV), "God said, 'Let us make man in our image.'" Thus, man was created by the word or words of God. To me, this is affirmed in Psalm 33:9 (RSV): "For he spoke, and it came to be; he commanded, and it stood forth."

From this understanding of the spoken word came blessings and curses. Ancient blessings were spoken words that benefitted the receiver, and spoken curses carried a negative consequence. We see this during the time of Jesus. In Mark 11 is the brief story of Jesus and a fig tree. Jesus, along with the twelve disciples, were traveling from Bethany. Jesus was hungry and saw a fig tree, but discovered it had no figs. In response, Jesus said, "May no one ever eat fruit from you again" (Mark 11:14b NRSV). The story continues in verses 20 and 21, saying, "In the morning as they passed by, they saw the fig tree withered away to its roots. Then Peter remembered and said to him, 'Rabbi, look! The fig tree that you cursed has withered.'"

In Matthew 7:21, Jesus says, "Not everyone who says to me, 'Lord, Lord,' shall enter the kingdom of heaven." What Jesus says is that spoken words can be empty and meaningless. Empty words carry no power or influence. However, words spoken from a heart of faith can touch people, change people, and give people hope.

However, Jesus goes on to state that no one goes to heaven "but he who does the will of my father who is in heaven." As Jesus says, empty words will not change things but words that come from faith which is felt and lived can change the lives of others.

Even in our world today, a kind word can lift the spirit of the recipient, and a negative word can bring despair.

SAYING 12

"Take heart, my son; your sins are forgiven."
—Matthew 9:2b (RSV)

JESUS SAYS THIS to a paralytic who could not walk. There was a crowd of people present when Jesus addressed the paralytic, and inside the crowd were several scribes. Within the community of Jewish religious leaders were those who were forever watching what Jesus was doing and what he was saying. Thus, they would try to discredit him. Anyone who spoke differently or behaved differently from the speech and actions of the Jewish religious leaders was considered in the wrong and evil. Jesus did not initially say, "Arise and go home," but he said, "Take heart, my son; your sins are forgiven." This statement angered the scribes. However, if Jesus had said initially, "Rise and go home," they would have criticized him anyway. Why? Because Jesus was not a part of their group and anything or anyone outside of their group was wrong and evil. Jesus then said to the paralytic, "Rise, take up your bed and go home (9:6)

What a miserable life these religious leaders must have lived. They thought they were the authorities of Judaism and anything that deviated from their teachings and their conduct was wrong. Thus, they were forever looking at everyone and everything else to find the wrong and the evil. With such a negative mindset, they failed to see the good in the world, the good in many people, and the good in Jesus.

I am sure they missed the pleasure of a friendly hello from a stranger. I am sure they missed the laughter of a group of children playing in the outdoors. I am sure they missed the smile of a young lady. I am sure they missed the touch of a baby's hand. I am sure they missed the beauty of the setting sun. I am sure they missed the love of a family gathering. I am sure they missed the praise from their grandfathers. I am sure they missed the grace of a loving God.

SAYING 13

"For I came not to call the righteous, but sinners."
—Matthew 9:13 (RSV)

THIS VERSE FOLLOWS the earlier verses in Matthew chapter 9, in which Jesus healed a paralytic and called a tax collector named Matthew to follow him. Jesus meant for Matthew to learn from him and be one of his disciples. The last event before 9:13 was a dinner where tax collectors and sinners attended so they could hear his message, ask questions, and learn from him.

The Pharisees had become aware of this meeting between Jesus and these undesirable people. Jesus heard the words of the Pharisees and responded by saying, "Those who are well have no need of a physician, but those who are sick" (Matthew 9:12 RSV) do.

What did Jesus mean by this statement? Jesus says that people know when they are sick; therefore, they need a physician. People who are not ill know that they do not need a physician. In essence, Jesus says that these undesirable people know they are spiritually sick. They know they are distant from God. They understand that they do not measure up to all the rules and rituals of the religious elite. They are very much aware that they are sinners. They want to know if there is any hope for them. They know they are unworthy.

The Pharisees, on the other hand, think they are righteous. They think they are close to God as determined by the rules and rituals of the Jewish faith. They believe they are worthy in God's eyes. They know, they think, that if all the other Jews followed their example, listen to their teachings, followed their rituals, and mimicked their conduct, then they would also be worthy. In addition, if they were worthy in God's eyes, they would prosper. With all this in mind, what did Jesus mean when he said that he came for sinners? Jesus says that he came not to call those who thought they were righteous. Those were the ones who looked down on the common people, and those who would never consider themselves sinners. Jesus says he came for sinners, those who knew they were sinners but earnestly desired to know and experience the love of God, the forgiveness of God, the peace of God, and the hope of God for them.

Those who thought they were righteous were not. Sinners knew they were not righteous, but they desired to be righteous. They wanted to be loved, to be forgiven, and to be eternally blessed.

Jesus had that love for them. He had that forgiveness for them, and eternal blessings for them as well.

SAYING 14

"Come to me, all who labor and are heavy laden,
and I will give you rest. Take my yoke upon you,
and learn from me; for I am gentle and lowly
in heart, and you will find rest for your souls.
For my yoke is easy and my burden is light."

—Matthew 11:28–30 (NKJV)

THIS MEMORABLE SAYING of Jesus is not an easy one to understand. Perhaps one of the best ways to approach this saying is to ask who the audience is. Jesus does not tell us right off who the audience is, which would greatly help us understand this seemingly difficult saying.

Today, the audience could be people who are elderly, people who are retired, people who have worked hard all their adult lives, people who are just getting by with their retirement income, and people who know they do not have many more years to live. This passage can be very helpful and meaningful to them, for they are tired, they have suffered, and they do not see much to celebrate for the few years left. To these, Jesus says, from me you will find rest for your souls. Jesus offers them a lighter load. With Jesus's help, with Jesus's grace, with Jesus's forgiveness, and with Jesus's assurance of life eternal, the load indeed is lighter, and the worry is less. This Jesus offers to senior citizens today, but also to anyone else who will listen.

As for the audience in verses 25 through 27, Jesus seems to have exposed those individuals. He also exposed the source of the heavy burden. There are two groups in these verses. One is the "wise and understanding," which means those who see themselves as the "wise and understanding"—the Jewish religious leaders. They continually tell the common people, the working people, that they are not living by all the laws and teachings that God demands. They say, "Thank God I am not like them."

The other group is those Jesus referred to as babes, or the unlearned. It is very interesting to note that shepherds worked every day tending their sheep. Therefore, they violated the Sabbath laws, which the religious leaders told them displeased God. However, it was to these shepherds—these working people, these unlearned people, these people rejected by the religious leaders—that God sent an angel, who told them "for to you is born this day in the city of David a Savior, who is Christ the Lord" (Luke 2:11 RSV). Therefore, Jesus was speaking to the working people, those rejected people, those "poor in spirit," and telling them, "Come to me, all who labor and are heavy laden, and I will give you rest."

SAYING 15

"A sower went out to sow."
—Matthew 13:3b (RSV)

THIS STATEMENT BEGINS Jesus's Parable of the Sower. Rather than discuss the parable itself, though it has much to teach us, I want to look at this sentence and see what the Lord would have us learn. The sower went out to sow. Why? Because that is who he was and what he did.

I believe individuals truly need to know who they are, or what they are. About three years ago, I was a patient in one of our hospitals here in the Nashville, Tennessee area. I was waiting in the surgery unit when a physician entered and introduced himself to me. He told me that he was to be my anesthesiologist. He said in humor that he would be the one keeping me alive. We then began to discuss his role in this procedure. After a while, I asked him, "Why are you not retired?"

He replied that he had already retired; however, he did not like it. When he retired from the hospital, he went home, sat in his favorite chair, and read the paper. Days came and days went, and he was very displeased. One day after he had been retired for several weeks, he decided this was not the life for him. He went back to the hospital and asked for his job back. The hospital quickly put him back to work. We talked about that, and he concluded saying, "I am an anesthesiologist. I like what I do, and it gives my life purpose and meaning."

Another experience I had happened about a year ago. I was visiting a college campus here in our area. My purpose was to talk to the business department and, more especially, the computer area. I was trying to learn from them what all they covered in preparing a student for a career in computers. I was introduced to one of their computer professors, who would be more able to discuss that topic than several others. The discussion went well; yet, during some of his presentation, I had almost no knowledge of what he was saying. However, I became convinced that when a student finished his or her studies, that person would step into the world well-equipped for computer work. When our discussion about computers ended, I asked him how much longer he was going to work there at the college. To my question, he replied, "Oh, I have already retired once. However, I was miserable. In a short amount of time, I came to realize that I am a computer professor. That is what I am and that is what I love. I came back to the college and asked for my job back. In turn, they accepted me back."

In reference to the above passage, Christians need to know who they are. As Christians, we are Christ's followers. That is what we are. We walk in his footsteps, and that is our task every day and all day. We live according to his teachings, his character, and his grace. I am truly convinced that many people who call themselves Christians do not know or understand what being a Christian really is. Jesus expects a lot out of his followers. I believe one of the clearest statements about what Christ expects comes from his own lips when he said, "Love the Lord your God with all your heart, with all your soul, and with all your mind." He also added, "Love your neighbor as yourself." What is this saying? Jesus expects his followers to truly love God and truly love other people.

SAYING 16

"Again, the kingdom of heaven is like a merchant in search of fine pearls, who, on finding one pearl of great value, went and sold all that he had and bought it."

—Matthew 13: 45–46 (RSV)

THIS PARABLE OF Jesus is rather brief. I do wish he had given us more information so that we possibly could see or understand more clearly. What we do know is that it is about the kingdom of heaven. Jesus has given us a number of parables that begin with "The kingdom of heaven is like." That is our theme and what follows is a merchant, a pearl, and a purchase.

I believe what Jesus was trying to say is that the kingdom of heaven should be worth everything to us. Perhaps we have heard something like this in today's world. As a pastor several years ago, I performed many, many, funerals. I heard comments, like this one from an older man who had lost his wife to death: "I would give everything I have just to see her once more." Truly, she must have meant everything to him.

In one of the churches, I pastored a couple in their middle to late forties who had moved into our town and joined our church. The wife worked as a secretary and the husband was an engineer. I knew very little about their background, but I came to know them fairly well. One day, I was in the office where the wife worked and she made a comment that her husband engaged in conversation very little. She went to say that the reason was that he had headaches every day, all day long. He had these headaches all his life and the physicians had not been able to solve his problem. Following that, she said, "He would give everything he has to rid himself of the headaches." In our world, some things to some people are worth everything.

I see this passage saying that the kingdom of heaven should be worth everything. To me this passage is much like Matthew 6:33 (NKJV): "But seek you first the kingdom of God, and his righteousness, and all these things shall be added unto you." What that statement says is that the kingdom of God should be first in our lives.

P.S. The parable of the Pearl of Great Price was used by John Steinbeck in his novel *The Pearl.* I am very fond of this book, and I recommended it to my students when I was teaching at the college in Florida. In like manner, I recommend it to any of the readers of the *Memorable Sayings of Jesus.*

SAYING 17

"Woman, great is your faith!"
—Matthew 15:28 (NRSV)

THIS IS A very interesting story of a Gentile woman—a Canaanite—and Jesus. At first reading, one usually feels that Jesus has no concern or feelings for this woman, who was pleading with him to heal her daughter who was tormented by a demon. First, Jesus did not respond to her plea. Then why did she continue to ask? To me, she sounds like a mother who greatly loves her daughter. She would endure the embarrassment, and the ridicule, for the sake of her child. This woman was much like many, many, mothers in that she would do most anything to save the child she brought into the world. She shouted at Jesus, she got on her knees before Jesus, and she continued to beg him to heal her child. She even called him Lord.

I believe Jesus knew what was inside this woman; he knew of her determination, and he already knew what he was going to do. I believe Jesus wanted the disciples to see how much she loved her child, how determined she was to continue her efforts, and how much faith she had in Jesus's ability to heal. Thus, Jesus responded by saying, "Woman, great is your faith! Let it be done for you as you wish."

What were the results of this encounter between Jesus and the Gentile woman? First, the disciples walked away with a different understanding of Jesus. Second, the mother walked away with a joyful heart. And third, the child walked away, or was carried away, with a new life. What then can we say? Thank you, Jesus, for caring.

SAYING 18

"But who do you say that I am?"
—Matthew 16:15b (NRSV)

IN THIS ENCOUNTER with his disciples, Jesus poses the question, "Who do people say that the Son of Man is?" This is a legitimate question by Jesus to find out what people throughout the land were saying about him. Jesus might be wondering if the people understood his feeding of the 5,000, his healing of the lame, his restoring sight to the blind, his teachings of love for one's neighbor, and his rejection of the false teaching of the Pharisees and Sadducees. However, the disciples' answer did not reflect on how well they understood him. "But who do you say that I am?" Jesus might be asking, "You that follow me daily, do you understand me? Do you understand what I am saying?" To this Peter replied, "You are the Christ, the son of the living God" (Matthew 16:16 NKJV). Yes, Jesus got the right answer from Peter. Peter's statement was absolutely correct. However, did he truly understand the magnitude of Jesus as the Christ, the son of God? If so, how could Peter ever deny Jesus three times (Matthew 26:69–75)?

Can we ever in our day truly understand Jesus? To say that in another way, can we understand God? Is not God so greatly divine that we can hardly understand what divine is actually like? Can we understand all the sayings of Jesus? It was Jesus who said, "Be perfect, therefore, as your heavenly Father is perfect" (Matthew

5:48 NIV). What all does this mean? There is no way for us to be perfect when we know in truth that we are sinners. Paul told us that in Romans 3:23b (NIV): "all have sinned and fall short of the glory of God."

Another passage that is very difficult to handle is Luke 6:27–28 (NRSV), in which Jesus says, "But I say to you that listen, love your enemies, do good to those who hate you, bless those who curse you, and pray for those who abuse you." I am sure Jesus said that, but I am also sure that most all of us do a poor job of upholding that command. Can I love someone who would abuse my wife, or my sons, or my grandchildren? I do not believe I can do that.

Another equally difficult passage is Matthew 22:37 (NKJV). Jesus said, "You shall love the Lord your God with all your heart, and with all your soul, and with all your mind." How do we do that? How can we love God with all that we are? Does that mean that we must keep our minds upon God every minute of the day? Jesus does not really tell us how to do that. How can we keep our minds on God every moment when we have jobs, families that need our attention, and relationships with other people to maintain? I do not see how we can measure up to that statement.

However, I do not believe a full understanding of Jesus is possible for us. Jesus is far more loving, far more caring, and far more holy than we are. However, Jesus does not require us to fully understand him. He requires that we believe in him, love him, and commit our lives to him.

SAYING 19

"If any man would come after me, let him deny
himself and take up his cross and follow me."
—Matthew 16:24b (RSVP)

JESUS SAID THESE words to his disciples. The disciples cherished these words, as do many Christians today. This passage continues to be preached, taught, and shared with others because it simply states Jesus's expectations of his followers.

Jesus was voicing this statement directly to his disciples. They were the ones on whom he relied on to tell the world who he was and that he could change people's lives.

To understand discipleship, one must first need to know what a disciple is. The term *disciple* means a follower of an individual, and more specifically, a believer in the teachings of that person.

This saying breaks into several notable parts. The first part is composed of the words, "If any man would come after me." What was Jesus saying? To me the wording of that is not very clear. I like *The Anchor Bible* translation much better which states, "If anyone will come with me." This statement clearly states that Christianity and discipleship is a free choice. To follow Christianity, or any other world religion, is a choice made in the heart of an individual. Even in parts of the world where a certain religion is forced on the people, deep in the heart is where true faith dwells. For Christians, that faith centers on Jesus Christ. However, Jesus expects obedience from his followers. God has created us to be free and free to choose our own faith.

Having taught the various religions of the world for many years, and having met and talked with many, many followers of other religions, I came to understand most of these people affirm that true religion is a choice of the heart.

The second part is a call to a follower to "let him deny himself." What was Jesus saying? He was saying deny yourself thoughts, words, and actions which violate the teachings of Jesus, such as, hatred, greed, lust, infidelity, racism, bitterness, anger, theft, gossip, lying, self-centeredness, and the list goes on. If Christ is who we are following, then we are to live and act like him, which means practicing kindness, forgiveness, love, understanding, prayer, acceptance, and concern for others.

The third part is an instruction that a follower should "take up his cross." Is Jesus talking about dying for him? Maybe, but I think not because the disciples did not know of Jesus's pending death on the cross at that time. Jesus had not mentioned it to them yet. That came later. "Take up his cross" sounds like a common phrase used by the public at large, which meant to carry the weight and responsibility of a given task, much like a criminal who carries the heavy load of his cross when he goes to his execution. In Luke's gospel, he wrote that Jesus said that a follower should "take up his cross daily" (Luke 9:23 NKJV). Followers today are to carry the weight and responsibility of whatever task that Jesus has given them.

The last part is a call to "follow me." That is what Jesus wanted and expected from his disciples. That is what Jesus wants and expects out of his followers today as well. Following Jesus is not something we say we do, but something we truly do throughout our Christian lives.

Therefore, Jesus has given us a more complete understanding of what it means to be his disciple, or stated in other words, what it means to be a Christian. Discipleship means obedience and service; however, the rewards of a life of faith and joy are worth every minute of it.

SAYING 20

"The Son of man is to be delivered into
the hands of men, and they will kill him,
and he will be raised on the third day."

—Matthew 17: 22–23 (NASB)

THE TEXT REVEALS that the disciples were greatly distressed when they heard this. Well, why would they not be? Their hopes and dreams of a Messiah, in their eyes, had come true. His teachings, his healings, his miracles, his compassion, and his wisdom clearly indicated that he was the Messiah. This happened during their lifetime. They were able to hear him, talk with him, and enjoy his presence. For 400 years, the people of Israel longed for a new prophet who spoke the words of God, but there were no new words from God. However, now that new message from God was in their midst. Their longing for a message from God had come true in their lifetime. What joy, what excitement, and what a blessing. However, Jesus was saying he would die at the hands of men and be raised on the third day. Why? Why would that happen? The joy was too great to come to an end. They had waited 400 years for this holy man, and now he would be gone. No wonder they were greatly distressed. We too can sense their sorrow. We too can raise the same question. Why? However, these disciples did not know the rest of the Jesus story at that time. How could they? They had heard him, they had watched him, but they had not seen the depths of his love for them and others. He died because he loved them more than they could understand. In addition, his love was not only for them, but for everyone. Even today, his great love is still with us.

SAYING 21

"Who is the greatest in the kingdom of heaven?"
—Matthew 18:1b (NRSV)

"Whoever becomes humble like this child is
the greatest in the kingdom of heaven."
—Matthew 18:4 (NRSV)

THESE TWO PASSAGES focus on Jesus and children. In fact, there are several such passages in the Gospels regarding Jesus and children. These include Mark 9:37, Matthew 19:13–15, and Matthew 21:16. In this second passage, Jesus said, "Whoever becomes humble like this child is the greatest in the kingdom of heaven." For us adults, there is a problem with this text. Jesus used the child as a model of humility. We adults will not hold to that idea, and I believe we cannot hold to it. Why? Because we have our egos with which to contend. We have responsibilities that pull us into a secular and sinful world that hinders us. We are sinners, which impedes our humility; children are not. Jesus says to us that the children are the greatest in the kingdom of God.

Think about that. We attribute greatness to wealth, power,

popularity, brilliance, success, and the list goes on. Children have none of that. In fact, we attribute in our society very little value to children. Many times, we send our children to childcare centers so that parents can work all day. Childcare workers who oversee our children usually are paid lower wages than many working-class people. In addition, many children throughout our country go to bed each night hungry. Another point is that many people in this country holler, "No! Abortions!" "No! Abortions!" but say very little concerning children being abused by their parents, or their teachers, or childcare workers, or their ministers. We regularly read in our papers of children being chained to their beds, children being beaten, children being burned with cigarettes, children being forced into sexual activities by adults, and the list goes on. Nevertheless, Jesus said children are the humble ones, and the greatest in the kingdom of God.

Oh God, help us to view children and value children as you do.

SAYING 22

"'My house shall be called a house of prayer':
but you are making it a den of robbers."
—Matthew 21:13b (NRSV)

JESUS MADE THAT statement when he entered the temple
of God, and drove out those who were buying and selling, and
exchanging currency for a profit. It is true that many people in
Jerusalem did not care if such activities were occurring because
they were occurring in the court of the Gentiles. They had no
concern about Gentiles worshiping God anyway. However, Jesus
cared. The temple of God was for all who chose to worship the
God of the Jews. The entire area of the temple was made for prayer,
worship, praise, meditation, and communing with God. I know
we can worship God anywhere. I know God will hear our worship
wherever we are located. However, is there no value in dedicating
a building, a piece of land, a location, or a place, solely for the
purpose of worship and prayer? Many religions throughout the
world have special places of worship, ritual, prayer, and meditation,
such as mountains, rivers, valleys, or buildings. Is there no value
in having a sacred place dedicated to the worship of God, which is
not used for business meetings, political speeches, secular concerts,

worldly debates, and entertainment? Perhaps our worship would have more meaning, more feeling of God's presence, more of a sense of the sacred, if we dedicated church sanctuaries to God for the purpose of worship. I believe that would take us closer to the throne of God.

SAYING 23

"Render therefore to Caesar the things that are Caesar's and to God the things that are God's."
—Matthew 22:21b (NKJV)

THE QUESTION THAT was placed before Jesus was, "Is it lawful to pay taxes to Caesar, or not?" This is an interesting passage, for it appears that Jesus had very little to say about politics or government. Why, one would ask? Are not government and politics very important in the existence of civilization? Do we not see in our society preachers inviting certain politicians into their pulpits during the season of elections? These politicians may share their testimony about their Christian raising leading to their Christian faith. They may even lead prayers asking for God's blessings. Thus, a number of preachers are invited to the White House, and have their pictures taken while they shake the hand of the president and other politicians. Is this not the norm in our society? Why was Jesus so lax about discussing politics? Why did Jesus say to give to Caesar what was Caesar's and to God what was God's?

Jesus knew that civility in society was far better for everyone than chaos and anarchy. In order for government and civility to exist, the government must be supported by the people. It takes money to maintain a government. That is part of the reason Jesus said what he did. However, the second part of the reason is that Jesus saw his job, his calling, his commitment as more important than being sidetracked into politics. Ministering to the needs of people and giving them life, peace, joy, love, hope, healing, and salvation is far more important than talking politics. Jesus was totally committed to his ministry. I believe preachers and churches have a far greater task: to minister to people, love people, provide food for the hungry, aid the poor, visit the sick, befriend the lonely, lift up the fallen, and preach and teach of the love and redemption of Jesus Christ. Churches ought to get out of politics and do the work of Christ Jesus.

SAYING 24

He said to them "You shall love the Lord your God with all your heart, and with all your soul, and with all your mind. This is the greatest and first commandment. And a second is like it: You shall love your neighbor as yourself."

—Matthew 22:37–38 (ESB)

PARALLEL PASSAGES

"You shall love the Lord your God with all your heart, and with all your soul, and with all your mind, and with all your strength." (Mark 12:30–31 ESB)

"You shall love the Lord your God with all your heart, and with all your soul, and with all your strength, and with all your mind." (Luke 10:27a ESB)

A lawyer asked Jesus which commandment in the law was the greatest. Jesus replied by saying, "You shall love the Lord your God with all your heart, and with all your soul, and with all your mind. This is the greatest and first commandment." In Judaism, this is known as the *Shema,* and it is found in Deuteronomy 6:4–5. The

Jews were to recite this twice a day: once in the morning and once in the evening.

This is a very difficult passage. Most all Christians know this saying of Jesus. They also think that this statement is what most Christians and church members do. However, do church members truly love God with all their hearts, souls, and minds? If the answer is yes, then how much time do they spend daily in Bible study and prayer? How many people in a day do they tell that God truly loves them? When Jesus said to love "with all your heart, soul, and mind," he meant with the totality of our lives. Can we even do that? I think not. I think what Jesus was saying that even though, as sinners, we cannot do that, he expects us to continue trying throughout our lives. That is what being a Christian is.

The second part is to love your neighbor as yourself. Again, I ask: do we love others? Many Christians love their neighbors, as evidenced by what they do. They feed the hungry, give the thirsty something to drink, welcome strangers, clothe the naked, and visit the sick. For Jesus said, "Truly I tell you, just as you did it to one of the least of these who are members of my family, you did it to me" (Matthew 25:40b NRSV).

No, we are not perfect. We still have a distance to go to be completely committed. Yes, we try to do the things that help others. We do this because we love our Lord, who first loved us (1 John 4:19).

SAYING 25

"Beware that no one leads you astray."
—Matthew 24:4b (NRSV)

TALKING TO HIS disciples about the temple in Jerusalem, Jesus said that "not one stone will be left here upon another; all will be thrown down."

He was preparing them for the lead-up to the end time. He was also warning them about false prophets who would lead many people astray. Jesus was concerned that his message and ministry would continue to transform the lives of people until the very end. Jesus's disciples needed to hear this, and so do people today. Let no one lead a person of faith astray. How often do we read about a Christian minister caught being unfaithful to his or her spouse? How often do we read about priests or church officials sexually abusing the children in the church? How often do we read about ministers preaching a hate message to their church members? How often do we read of church officials embezzling money from the church? These activities destroy the image and ministry of the Christian church. However, somewhat the same can be said about an individual who claims to be a Christian and embezzles money, cheats on their taxes, tells dirty jokes, gets caught with a prostitute, is drunk or on drugs in public, or tries to seduce his or her neighbor's spouse.

I have young grandchildren and I have been teaching them a prayer that I want them to recite several times a day. The prayer is,"

Lord Jesus, lead my life." I believe if they recite this prayer and let it be a guide for their lives, then their Christian light will shine, and they will be committed followers of Christ Jesus. A simple prayer can change a person's life.

SAYING 26-A

"I was hungry and you gave me food."
—Matthew 25:35a (NRSV)

IN THIS PASSAGE, Jesus refers to the Great Judgment, in which he separates the sheep from the goats. Jesus will say to those at his right hand, "Come, you that are blessed by my Father, inherit the kingdom prepared for you from the foundation of the world; for I was hungry and you gave me food" (Matthew 25:34b–35a NRSV). Jesus also mentions being a stranger, being naked, being sick, and being in prison, and being ministered to in all those situations. However, others did not minister to his needs. The people asked Jesus when they failed to minister to him. Jesus replied, "Truly, I tell you just as you did not do it to one of the least of these, you did not do it to me. And these will go away into eternal punishment, but the righteous into eternal life" (Matthew 25:45b NRSV).

In most of our churches, we hear songs, prayers, and sermons about salvation, faith, belief in Christ, sharing the gospel, and witnessing to lost people. All of this is good, and it is biblical. We have Bible verses that relate directly to these words, such as John 3:16, Ephesians 2:8–9, 1 John 1:9, and many more. However, that is not the complete picture. Yes, faith in Christ is essential to becoming a Christian, but becoming a Christian is only the beginning of our Christian pilgrimage. Years ago, I heard an old preacher say, "Christianity is what we do." I never forgot that statement, even though I never truly understood what it meant either. As the years have gone by, I have come to understand what he meant. He meant what Jesus said. Feed the hungry. As Christians, Christ gave us a task to minister to the needs of people. Faith then is what we do, faith is what we say, and faith is how we love others. Faith is feeding the hungry and caring for the sick; faith is doing what Jesus did and living like Jesus lived. James was correct when he wrote, "So faith by itself, if it has no works [no ministry, no loving, no caring for others], is dead" (James 2:17 NRSV).

SAYING 26-B

"I was hungry, and you gave me food."
—Matthew 25:35a (NRSV)

"I was hungry and you gave me no food."
—Matthew 25:42a (NRSV)

THESE TWO PASSAGES are very much alike, except that the first passage is stated in the positive while the second passage is stated in the negative. Jesus continued by saying that those who do not give food to the hungry "will go away into eternal punishment, but the righteous into eternal life."

Back in November 2019, Sandy, my wife, and I went to the Meijer's store in Hilliard, Ohio, to purchase some needed items. Later, as we were leaving in our car, we pulled up next to an elderly woman of short stature as she stood there next to the exit of the parking lot. She had a cardboard sign that stated she was homeless. In response, we gave her some money, we spoke God's blessing upon her, and drove away. When we do give to those who ask we never ask them how they will use it. Why? It is not for us to know. Jesus never said, "Make sure you ask so they will not buy alcohol nor drugs." Jesus said to give. When it leaves my hand and goes to her hand, then it is hers. If she uses it in an inappropriate way, then she will have to answer for that to Christ Jesus when her days are over.

Therefore, we do not worry, we do not speculate; we have done what the Good Lord tells us to do.

Several years ago, when I was teaching at the college in Orlando, I had left the campus to go over to a small shopping area not far from the campus. As I pulled into the parking lot, I saw a man who was tall and thin and probably around twenty-five years of age standing there with a sign. With him was a little girl, probably six years of age. I parked my car and walked over to where he was, we talked briefly, and I gave him some money and walked away. It was enough money to feed him and her for the noon meal. A little later, I left the shopping area and made my way back to campus. Later that day, I went back to the same shopping area for another reason, and I pulled into the parking lot. When got out, I noticed the man was on the asphalt with a police officer over him, putting handcuffs on him. The little girl was not there. I do not know why that happened. However, I did not question if I did the right thing in giving him money. If he were not an honest person, if he were guilty of some crime, I do not know. That is between him and the Lord Jesus. I give because the Lord gives to us.

One other story might be of interest. About two weeks ago, my wife and I left home, heading west of Nashville, Tennessee. While ramping off Interstate 70, I noticed a young man, probably twenty to twenty-five years of age, with a sign. My wife said to me that there was a young man in need. I could not stop and get out of the car because cars were lining up behind me. I drove across the street into a small shopping area. I got out of the car and walked back across the street to talk to the young man as he stood there waiting for help. He was a very friendly person with a smile on his face. I asked him how well he was doing. He responded that he was doing fairly well, for one person had given him four dollars and another person had given him fifteen cents. I knew that it was about noon, and he would need something to eat, so I handed him some money to help. Then I told him that the Lord had been good to me, and he expects me to be good to him. As I crossed the street and headed back to my car, I heard him holler at me and say with a grin on his face, "I do not drink alcohol and I do not smoke cigarettes."

In our world today, there are many people in need and the Good Lord is looking at us to be of help to them.

SAYING 27-A

"Why do you trouble the woman?"
—Matthew 26:10b (NRSV)

THIS EVENT HAPPENED during Jesus's last days. We can read about it in Matthew 26:6–10 (NRSV).

> Now when Jesus was at Bethany in the house of Simon the leper, a woman came up to him with an alabaster jar of very costly ointment, and she poured it on his head as he sat at the table. But when the disciples saw it, they were angry and said, "Why this waste? For this ointment could have been sold for a large sum, and the money given to the poor." Then Jesus replied, "Why do you trouble the woman?"

There is no doubt this woman's action was one of devotion to Christ. However, the men, Jesus's disciples, believed they had the right to evaluate this woman and tell her what she should have done.

This event was very indicative of the ancient world. However, it also reflects our world today. So many people spend so much time telling other people how to do a certain thing, how it should be done, how it could be improved, and how it should be corrected—all while they do very little. In this account, apparently the men were engaging in conversation, but they were actually doing very little.

They did nothing and freely told others what to do or what not to do. Instead of correcting and condemning others, we would do better if we looked into ourselves and corrected our own flaws. I believe we need to spend more time encouraging others and lifting them up, than putting them down and breaking their spirits.

SAYING 27-B

"Why do you trouble the woman?"
—Matthew 26:10 (NRSV)

AS MENTIONED ON the previous page, Jesus's statement chastises the disciples for complaining about what they perceived as a waste of expensive ointment. Jesus commended the woman for preparing his body for burial.

It is interesting to note that many commentaries do not include this memorable statement. Many of these commentaries discuss the value of the ointment and the concern for the poor, and assert that the woman will be remembered wherever the gospel is preached. I think these assessments miss a key point in the gospel of Jesus. Jesus rebuked the disciples for what they had said and done. This verse has been translated several different ways.

- "Why do you trouble the woman?" (RSV, NRSV)
- "Why do you distress this woman? (Barclay)
- "Why make trouble for this woman?" (REB)
- "Why are you bothering this woman?" (NIV)

There are perhaps others. However, I think in our vocabulary it would be stated, "Why are you abusing her?" or "Why are you trying to demean her?" or "Why are you putting her down?" I believe the statement of Jesus has a sharp edge to it. It was not an idle statement.

I believe Jesus saw the disciples rebuking her. Why? Because she was a woman. It is true that Jewish women were treated better in the ancient world than women of Greece or women of Rome. However, Hebrew men still did not see Hebrew women on the same level as they were. There are several examples throughout the Scriptures that seem to affirm that idea. I believe one example clearly presents that concept. Luke 24:10–11 tells the account of the women going to the tomb of Jesus and finding it empty. They went to the disciples to tell them that Jesus had risen. As Luke writes, "Now it was Mary Magdalene, Joanna, Mary the mother of James, and the other women with them who told this to the apostles. But these words seem to the men an idle tale, and they did not believe them."

Women of today are in somewhat the same position. Much of society does not see women on the same level as men. Women, like men, are created by God. Women, like men, are people of the kingdom of God. Women, like men, are very important in the eyes of God.

SAYING 28-A

"Truly, I say to you, one of you will betray me."
—Matthew 26:21b (NASB)

THESE ARE THE words of Jesus as he gathered with his disciples. He tells them that one of them would betray him to the Jewish leaders, and others who oppose him. Surely, shock went through the room. They wanted to know who would do such a terrible thing. At the same time, each began to ask himself if he could do that very act. Why would they question themselves? Was it because each one knew he was not as committed to Christ as he should have been, or as he seemed to be? Jesus's best friends were not sure whether they would or would not betray him.

Even Peter, who was the leader of the disciple fellowship, was probably questioning himself. He had reason to question himself, but he wanted to put on a good face by saying to Jesus, "Though all become deserters, because of you, I will never desert you" (Matthew 26:33b NRSV). To boost his ego he further, he said, "Even though I must die with you, I will not deny you" (Matthew 26:35b NRSV). Yet, a few hours later, Peter was accused of being with Jesus of Nazareth and in anger Peter replied, "I do not know the man" (Matthew 26:72b NRSV).

What do we gain from this account? What do we learn? As committed as we think we are, as devoted to Jesus as we believe we are, we too could possibly fall, as did Peter. Let it be known that

Jesus's closest friends, his disciples, failed to speak up on his behalf. They watched him die and they said nothing.

Whenever we think we are so strong in our faith that we would never deny Jesus, we should think for a minute how many "Christian"[6] ministers have abused small children. We should remember how many "Christian" people have cheated on their taxes and how many "Christian" people have been caught embezzling money. We should remember how many "Christian" politicians have lied to us to win elections. We should remember how many "Christian" husbands or wives have been unfaithful to their spouses. Remember, we are only people, but with Christ's help, we can overcome. Remember what the Lord said to Joshua, "I will not fail you or forsake you" (Joshua 1:5b NRSV).

That promise is still with us today.

---

[6] I use "Christian" means those who claim to be Christian.

SAYING 28-B

"Truly I say to you, one of you will betray me."
—Matthew 26:21b (NASB)

JESUS MADE THIS statement in the upper room just prior to the Last Supper. His disciples were with him, and they were eating the Passover meal. Jesus was very much aware that his time on earth was coming to a close, and he knew that "one of you will betray me." These twelve men were his friends, his followers, his students, and his daily companions over the three years of his ministry. Did Jesus not know who the betrayer was? Yes, he knew. This story bothers us because Judas was one of those companions. How could he have done that? He sided with the Jewish officials to arrest Jesus and ultimately kill him. We in the church are quick to condemn Judas and heap angry words on what he did. How could he do such a thing? Many of us see Judas as evil and deserving of his own death.

Well, someone else there also betrayed him. When a person violates the teachings of Jesus and violates the character of Jesus, that person also betrays the Jesus who loves us. Peter betrayed Jesus. At the arrest of Jesus, a woman approached Peter and said, "'You are not also one of this man's disciples, are you?' Peter replied, 'I am not'" (John 18:17b NRSV). Is that not betrayal? Is that not violating the teachings of Jesus? Is that not violating the character of Jesus? Yes indeed, that is betrayal.

It is easy for us to point at Judas, and it is easy for us to point at Peter. However, it is also true that when we do not live up to the teachings of Jesus and claim to be a Christian, we also betray him.

Jesus said to his disciples, "This is my commandment, that you love one another as I have loved you" (John 15:12 NRSV). When we violate Jesus's commandment of love, we betray him. When we despise the immigrant, we betray him. When we berate others, we betray him. When we detest the beggar on the street, we betray him. When we ridicule the poor, we betray him. When we are unkind, uncaring, and unconcerned for others, we too are the betrayers.

Lord, help us to not betray nor deny you, and please forgive us for when we do.

SAYING 29

"My Father, if it is possible, let
this cup pass from me."
—Matthew 26:39b (NRSV)

WHAT WAS THE answer to Jesus's prayer in the garden of Gethsemane? In Matthew 7:7, Jesus said, "Ask, and it will be given you; seek, and you will find; knock, and it will be opened to you." With that information, what did God say to Jesus?

Jesus's prayer is "My Father, let this cup pass from me." Mark's gospel gives us a better understanding of what Jesus meant by this cup." Mark 14:35 states that Jesus asks if "the hour might pass from him." Jesus asks God to remove the hour, remove the moment, remove the agony. The human side of Jesus is truly evident in this moment. However, Jesus continues to ask for "not what I want, but what you want." The latter part of the prayer reflects his faith, his commitment, and his dedication to the Father. This was a struggle for Jesus, because he voiced this prayer three times.

What then did God say to Jesus? The truth is we do not know. Why? Because in the wisdom of God, he deemed it right that we do not know. As I have mentioned before, there is much about God that we do not know. In fact, there is a lot in the Bible about God and from God that we still do not understand. For example, why is the Song of Solomon in the Bible? I really do not know. Why is the Revelation of John so difficult to understand? I do not know.

What I do know is that God is far more intelligent than we are, far more loving, far wiser, far more caring, and far more divine. God says in Isaiah 55:8, "For my thoughts are not your thoughts, neither are your ways my ways." The difference is that God is God, and we are only people.

SAYING 30

"My God, my God, why have you forsaken me?"
—Matthew 27: 46b (NRSV)

JESUS SPOKE THESE words while in great agony on the cross. The multitude had rejected him, ridiculed him, and made all kinds of remarks to humiliate him. While suffering severe pain, Jesus felt abandoned and scorned. Thus, he cried out, "My God, my God, why have you forsaken me?" This was truly the darkest hour for the Christ, who loved all the people yet was rejected by them.

The major point is that was how Jesus felt. He felt alone, he felt rejected, he felt pain, he felt that God had turned his back on him. Most all of us at times have moments of feeling rejected or abandoned. This is true when we lose our spouses to death, a son or daughter is killed in the military, a brother or sister or dear friend ends his or her own life, and maybe to a different degree, when our spouses walk away from us or have been unfaithful to us.

All these moments are extremely painful. Like Jesus on the cross, he felt God had forsaken him. However, we may feel that and believe that, but it is not true. If we know God, he is always with us. Life is hard at times, but God is always there. How do I know that?

It is the LORD who goes before you. He will be with you; he will not fail you nor forsake you. Do not fear or be dismayed. (Deuteronomy 31:8 NRSV)

"No one shall be able to stand against you all the days of your life. As I was with Moses, so I will be with you; I will not fail you or forsake you." (Joshua 1:5 NRSV)

Keep your lives free from the love of money, and be content with what you have; for he has said, "I will never leave you or forsake you." (Hebrews 13:5 NRSV)

Therefore, regardless of the tragedy or how we feel, God is always there, and God will always care.

SAYING 31

Then Jesus cried again with a loud
voice and breathed his last.
—Matthew 27:50 (NRSV)

I AM VERY much aware that this verse is not a quotation from the lips of Jesus. However, this verse has much to say. This is the verse that tells us of the very moment when Jesus died. I am sure many of the readers of this book have been with someone special when that person breathed his or her last. The very moment of death is the end of life here on earth. That moment is accompanied by great sorrow. Why? Because a love relationship has been broken. Life is precious. It is a gift from God, and we need to live it in honor of him who watches over us daily.

Nevertheless, how death comes, in many cases, is a mystery. Death can be brought on by illness, starvation, old age, war, car wrecks, accidents of all kinds, and numerous other causes. One way that bothers many people is when a friend, or relative, or a spouse, or someone else we love, commits suicide. Several years ago, as I pastored a church in South Carolina, a woman in our church had me notified that she was at the hospital because her son had committed suicide. I immediately went to the hospital to help comfort her in this time of great sorrow. I remember clearly what she asked of me: "Will my son go to hell because he committed suicide?" She then said, "I have heard all my life that people who committed suicide will go to hell. Is that true?" (I know that some religious fellowships hold to that teaching.) The concept that immediately came to my mind, which I shared with her, was as follows.

I said, "You know sometimes we sing the song, 'He Could Have Called Ten Thousand Angels.'[7] That song says that while Jesus was on the cross, he could have called ten thousand angels to take him off the cross, but he did not. Since he could have avoided death and did not, that is about as close to suicide as we can get. Jesus volunteered to die and that is what your son did. I do not believe Jesus will hold that against him."

Life is a gift and death is a mystery. However, even in death Jesus is still with us.

---

[7] Ray Overholt wrote the song "He Could Have Called Ten Thousand Angels," and he based it on Matthew 26:53.

SAYING 32

"All authority in heaven and on earth has been
given to me. Go therefore and make disciples
of all nations, baptizing them in the name
of the Father and of the Son and of the Holy
Spirit, and teaching them to obey everything
that I have commanded you. And remember, I
am with you always, to the end of the age."
—Matthew 28:18b–20 (NRSV)

NOW WE COME to the last memorable saying of Jesus in the
Gospel of Matthew. How is Matthew, under the inspiration of the
Heavenly Father, going to close out this book? Jesus said he had all
authority, and he was telling us to make disciples, baptize them,
and teach them, and he would be with us always even to the end of
the age.

What else can be said? What is left to be done? The disciples
heard his sermons, they listened to his teachings, they witnessed
his baptism, they saw him heal the sick and give sight to the blind,
they saw him on the cross, they went to the empty tomb, and they
greeted him as the risen Lord. What is left to do? Jesus saw that the
disciples needed to share what they saw him do, what they heard
him say, and what they experienced from being in his presence, with
others so the others could experience his saving grace and become

disciples as well. Jesus's work is not done. He wants faithful disciples to continue the work.

Now we close with a prayer. Lord Jesus, may you always find us as faithful disciples.

SAYING 33

The beginning of the gospel (*the good news*) of Jesus Christ, the Son of God.

—Mark 1:1 (NKJV)

THE FIRST STATEMENT I want to make about this saying is that it is not a saying from the mouth of Jesus Christ. I write about this saying because I think it is a wonderful quotation that has so much to say. My intent in writing this book is to limit myself to the sayings of Jesus that many people memorize and continue to quote throughout their lives. However, I violated my own intent because I think this quotation deserves to be considered.

In Mark 1:1 and following, the writer of this gospel, whether it was Mark the companion of Peter (1 Peter 5:13) or some other writer of God's choice, passed over the story of the birth of Jesus. To me this is amazing considering the importance of that story to the Christian church. Why was it left out?

Could the answer be that Mark did not know the story? Perhaps he never heard of the journey of Joseph and Mary from Nazareth to Bethlehem. Perhaps he had not heard of the shepherds in the field or the wise men. Is that the answer? I think not. Why? Mark, the companion of Peter, was a recipient of all the stories that Peter held. Some people see this gospel account as the gospel according to Peter as written by Mark. That makes sense to me.

Why then was it left out? That is like asking about the mind of God. Why does God allow things to happen such as floods, tornadoes, forest fires, diseases, and the like? Sometimes God intervenes in these events, like sending a hurricane back into the sea, and other personal events, like a person overcoming a deadly disease. Most every Christian can testify of some event when God intervened in that person's life. One such event is when a person experiences the forgiveness and salvation from Christ.

That story of the birth of Jesus is not in this gospel because of the wisdom of God. The heavenly father chose for it not to appear in the book of Mark. Why? That was his decision. Remember Isaiah 55:8 (NKJV): "For my thoughts are not your thoughts, nor are your ways my ways, says the Lord."

SAYING 34

"Let us go on to the next towns, that I may
preach there also; for that is why I came out."
—Mark 1:38b (RSV)

MARK 1:1–45 TELLS us the following. Jesus called Simon and
Andrew to follow him, and, shortly thereafter, he called James and
John. Then they went to Capernaum where he entered the synagogue
on the Sabbath. While in Capernaum he taught the people, he cast
out an unclean spirit, he healed Simon's mother-in-law of a fever, he
cast out demons, and he healed people of various diseases.

The next day, Simon and others searched for Jesus, who was
alone and praying. They found him and said to him, "Everyone is
searching for you." Then Jesus replied, "Let us go on to the next
towns, that I may preach there also; for that is why I came out."

What did he mean by the statement "that is why I came out"? He
might have meant that is why I left Capernaum. However, I think
he was saying that is why he came out to the people. That is why he
was with them, to give them the message of God.

His main focus was to preach to the people. Why? Because
the message has everlasting consequences such as peace, love,
forgiveness, and everlasting life. Jesus loved the people, he healed
the people, he taught the people, and all these activities were very
important. Therefore, these events remain with us in the here and
now. However, a message of God abides with us in the here and now,

and on through eternity. Why is preaching so important? It is the message of God.

A good example of a message from God that carries everlasting significance is in John 14:1–3 (NKJV). Jesus says,

> "Let not your hearts be troubled; you believe in God, believe also in Me. In my father's house are many mansions [rooms]; if it were not so, I would have told you. I go to prepare a place for you. And if I go and prepare a place for you, I will come again and receive you to Myself; that where I am, *there* you may be also. And where I go you know, and the way you know."

This sermon, or lesson, from Jesus is a message from God that has eternal significance.

SAYING 35-A

"I will; be clean."

—Mark 1:41b (RSV)

THIS SAYING, "I will; be clean" is found in the story of Jesus healing a man of leprosy. The man came to Jesus, knelt before him, and said, "If you will, you can make me clean." With pity, Jesus reached out his hand and touched him, and said, "I will; be clean." Immediately his leprosy was gone. This account is not only recorded in Mark, but also in Matthew 8:2–4 and Luke 5:12–16; these accounts are much the same.

In the Mark story, the author included a small phrase that the other two did not include. After healing the leper, Jesus "sent him away at once." This means that Jesus healed him immediately and then sent him away immediately. This story reminds me of Jesus healing the paralytic, as recorded in Mark 2, Matthew 9, and Luke 5. In this story, Jesus told the paralytic, "I say to you, rise, take up your pallet, and go home." The author then wrote, "And he rose, and immediately took up the pallet and went out before them all" (Mark 2: 11–12a). Thus, what we have in these two healing accounts is that Jesus healed them and immediately sent them away.

These two healing stories differ considerably from a number of other healing accounts, such as the healing of the ten lepers in Luke 17:11–19. These ten lepers asked Jesus to have mercy on them. Jesus told them, "Go and show yourselves to the priests." As they continued their journey, they noticed that they were cleansed. This was not an immediate healing. As they were journeying away from Jesus, the healing took place.

In John 9:1–12 is the story of a man born blind. Jesus spat on the ground, made mud with his saliva, and applied it to the man's eyes. Then Jesus said, "Go, wash in the pool of Siloam." After washing, the man returned to Jesus, able to see. In this case, much like the story of the ten lepers, the healing did not occur immediately. Why? Well, the biblical writers do not tell us. However, I am sure that Jesus did what he did, and said what he said, in the way and the time he deemed right. I believe that Jesus was far wiser, far more caring, and far more loving than we can ever understand.

I also believe that Jesus occasionally found himself in a moment that demanded immediate action. In other words, there are times when a decision or action needs to be made quickly. I believe that is true in our lives as well. This occurs in our secular lives as well is our religious lives. One such event as this occurred a number of years ago while I was pastoring in Greenville, North Carolina. One Sunday morning, a recently married couple visited our church. I tried to meet all our visitors as a courtesy, to get to know them and to see if there were any questions they had about our church. I also wanted to know if our church could assist them. In that regard, I talked with them about what Jesus could do for them in giving them a life of joy and meaning. As I began talking to them about Jesus, the young man said, "Pastor, you do not need to talk about this with me. The reason is that I am a Christian and have been for several years. But you do need to talk to her for she is not a Christian, and she wants to be." Therefore, I focused my attention on her, explaining from the Scriptures the love of Jesus, the forgiveness of Jesus, and the desire of Jesus to be within her. After this conversation, she bowed her head and prayed for Jesus to come into her life. After her prayer, I could see the joy and grace in her face. This was a moment in time in her life.

The next morning, she came by the church and I sat with her for a few moments and briefly discussed the events of the previous night. She was still excited. However, she was a schoolteacher and she, along with another schoolteacher, had to leave for a teacher's conference in Raleigh, North Carolina that day. As they traveled toward Raleigh, they were in a terrible automobile accident where she and her passenger both died immediately.

There are times when a decision needs to be made quickly. She made the decision because Jesus led her to that decision. Quickly, her life was taken away.

In the life of Jesus, a man with leprosy came to him and said, "If you will, you can make me clean." Jesus said, "I will; be clean." Immediately, he was cleansed and left Jesus. That was a moment in time when a quick decision was made. It was the right time for Jesus and for the leper.

SAYING 35-B

"I will; be clean."
—Mark 1:41b (RSV)

THE FOLLOWING IS another illustration of Christ intervening in a quick decision. Several years ago, when I was teaching at Valencia College in Orlando, Florida, I was on my way to the college in the midst of the morning traffic. The normal street that I traveled was a four-lane street that intersected another four-lane street. The other drivers and I were driving at a speed of about forty-five miles per hour, headed toward the intersection. As I quickly approached the intersection, I saw a young girl about twelve years of age standing on the sidewalk on the left side of the street. The cars in those lanes heading toward me were not moving. She ran across the lanes into the median. She stood in the median for a moment and then took off running across the right-hand lanes, headed for the other sidewalk. However, as she got in the middle of the second lane she turned and saw my car headed straight at her. At that moment she froze. I could see the fear in her face as my car headed toward her. I jerked the steering wheel to the right, veered the car into a right turn lane, and barely missed her. As I got by her and looked in the mirror, I could see her still standing frozen in the lane with the other cars stopping. As I went through the intersection, I realized that I almost hit and probably could have killed that young girl. The first thing I remember while going through the intersection was saying thank you Lord. The Lord helped me to make a quick decision and a life was saved. I have given thanks to the good Lord all these years for intervening in my life and saving hers.

SAYING 36

"See that you say nothing to anyone."
—Mark 1: 44b (RSV)

TWO VERSES IN this account of Jesus and the man with leprosy set the foundation of this biblical story. In Mark 1:44, Jesus tells the leper, "See that you say nothing to anyone." In Mark 1:45a (RSV), the writer tells us that the healed leper "went out and began to talk freely about it."

In this passage, the healed leper altered Jesus's plans. The leper came to Jesus "beseeching him, and kneeling said to him, 'If you will, you can make me clean'" (Mark 1:40b RSV). The text said Jesus was moved with pity, touched him, and he became clean. Jesus then told the healed leper, "See that you say nothing to anyone" (Mark 1:44b). However, the leper went out and talked freely about what Jesus had done for him.

Why is it important for us to look so carefully at this text? What we see is that Jesus had a plan to go to the towns throughout all Galilee. After the leper told people, "Jesus could no longer openly enter a town, but was out in the country" (Mark 1:45b RSV).

This means that Jesus's plans were drastically altered. He planned to visit the towns, but his plans had to be changed because of the leper's disobedience. That story relates to each one of us. God has a plan for each of us. It is our responsibility to discover that plan, or discover one step of God's plan, and be obedient.

God's plan for each person is apparent in the lives of the major characters in the Bible. One of those was the prophet Isaiah. He was a young person who had gone to the temple to worship. While he was there, he heard the voice of the Lord saying, "Whom shall I send, and who will go for us?" Isaiah said, "Here I am! Send me." God said, "Go, and say to this people" (Isaiah 6:8b–9a RSV). God had a plan for this young man, and he was obedient.

Another person for whom God had a plan was Jeremiah. Jeremiah says, "Now the word of the Lord came to me saying, 'Before I formed you in the womb I knew you, and before you were born I consecrated you; I appointed you a prophet to the nations'" (Jeremiah 1:4–5 RSV).

However, many times during our lives, we are not on target with God's plan for us. We make mistakes, we sin against him, we do not listen, we think we know a better way, and therefore, we violate God's plan for us. That does not mean that God is not with us. He knows that we are only people. Therefore, he alters his plans and puts us back on his course. Our major task, though, is to be obedient.

SAYING 37

"Little girl, I say to you, arise."
—Mark 5:41b (RSV)

THIS SAYING IS in Mark 5:21–24 and in Mark 5:35–43. This story is about Jairus, one of the rulers of the local synagogue, who went to Jesus to beg him to heal his daughter, who was at the point of death. Jairus believed, or hoped, that if Jesus laid his hands on her, she would become well. Jesus went with Jairus, took the child by her hand, and said, "'Little girl, I say to you, arise' and immediately she got up and walked" (Mark 4:41b–42a RSV).

What can we say about this story? Jesus healed numerous people. Yes! Jesus was seen by many people to be a compassionate person. Yes! Jesus was concerned about all kinds of people. Yes! However, I think the real focus of this story is that Jesus loved children. Jesus saw children as precious. In John 4:46, Jesus healed an official's son at Capernaum. In Matthew 15:28, Jesus healed the Canaanite woman's daughter. In addition, in Matthew 17:14, Jesus healed the epileptic boy.

Also in Mark 10:14–15 (RSV), Jesus said, "'Let the children come to me, do not hinder them; for to such belongs the kingdom of God. Truly, I say to you, whoever does not receive the kingdom of God like a child shall not enter it.' Then he took them in his arms and blessed them."

If children were precious to Jesus, they should also be that precious to us. Many people cherish children, but many do not. Years ago, while I was pastoring in Greenville, North Carolina, a couple in our church was expecting their first child. I was called from the church to go to their home and meet them there because their child was stillborn and the couple was devastated. My wife and I were parents of two boys, but never had we experienced such a trauma. However, my associate pastor and his wife had experienced a stillborn birth. As I was leaving the church, I asked him if he would go with me. He was a great help. He knew the heartache and pain of such an experience. He did a wonderful job listening to them, identifying with them, and consoling them.

Over the years of pastoring churches, many, many times I went to the hospitals to celebrate with a young couple and their newborn child. To them, a new child was precious.

However, there is the negative side. Numbers of children have been killed or greatly abused in our society. In 2017, 3,410 children and teens were killed with guns in America.[8] In 2020, at least six children on the Fourth of July were killed throughout this country as they played with friends outdoors, as they rode in their mothers' cars, and as they walked through malls.[9]

A recent news report stated that a thirty-two-year-old man had killed his own child who was five weeks old.[10] Along with these reports, we hear of children chained to their beds, locked in closets, beaten with belts, and burned with cigarettes.

---

[8] *Protect Children Not Guns Factsheet-2017 Child and Teen Gun Deaths*, accessed May 29, 2022, https://www.childrensdefense.org/wp-content/uploads/2019/05/2017-Child-and-Teen-Gun-Deaths.pdf

[9] Greg Norman, *4ᵗʰ of July Weekend Shootings Result in the Deaths of at least 6 Children*, Fox News. accessed May 29, 2022, https://www.foxnews.com/us/fourth-of-july-weekend-shootings

[10] *Father Charged with Murder in Death of 5-week-old Daughter*, Copyright 2021, City News Service, Inc. accessed May 29, 2022, fox5sandiego.com/news/local-news/father-charged-with-murder-in-death-of-5-week-old-daughter/

This list of children being killed or abused is in the news or on television most every night. Jesus, through his words and conduct, said children are precious. Why are they not more precious in our society?

SAYING 38

"Whoever causes one of these little ones who believe in me to sin, it would be better for him if a great millstone were hung around his neck, and he were thrown into the sea."

—Mark 9:42 (RSV)

IN SEVERAL PREVIOUS articles, I have discussed children. Jesus loved children and, children were precious in his eyes. In this article, I write again about children in the mind of Jesus. In our age, we read about children used as sexual objects, forced laborers, and drug peddlers. This was not God's plan for children, but what adults in our world have done to children. As children are loved and tended by Jesus, they should likewise be loved and cared for by us. One of the amazing things is what children do to adults. They remind us of what it was like when we were children. We remember when we chased after a ball with a stick, ate lima beans with our hands, caught and pet frogs, or picked up an acorn for the first time. We remember when we ran around in the yard chasing other children, rode on Dad's back like he was a horse, and got ice cream all over our faces. We remember the excitement of Christmas. We remember hiding in cardboard boxes, banging the pans under the kitchen sink, making mud pies with our hands, and many other experiences.

Jesus said that the people who abused children or caused them to sin should be attached to a millstone and thrown into the sea. In my feeling, there is no hell hot enough, no pain severe enough for these people. Children are God's gift and God's blessing to the world.

Years ago, when I was still a relatively young minister, I was asked by an older pastor to come to his church in the mountains of North Carolina and hold a series of services; we referred to this as a revival. While there, I was invited to visit a family for dinner. They were members of the church and were being very cordial. The older pastor told me that in the family was a father, a mother, a teenage daughter, and a baby that was less than a year old. The father of the newborn was not there. I was a bit anxious about that meeting for I would not know what to say. However, when the two of us entered the house, I was greatly surprised. Why? What I found was a teenage daughter who greatly loved her child and her parents. Her parents knew very well the mistake she had made. However, they greatly loved their daughter and their grandchild. The event was not awkward. It was joyful. I also was sorry for the mistake the young girl made, but I am sure that God smiled down on this child and this family.

In my mind, when Jesus talked about the millstone, he was on the edge of rage, much like he was when he cleansed the temple. The temple was designed and built to be a place of prayer and worship for all people, and they had made it into a place of commerce and secularism. Children were meant to be loved. Children were meant to be a blessing to this world.

SAYING 39

"Truly, I say to you, this poor widow has put
in more than all those who are contributing
to the treasury. For they all contributed out of
their abundance; but she out of her poverty has
put in everything she had, her whole living."

—Mark 12:43b-44 (RSV)

WATCHED THE RICH people placing large amounts of money in the temple treasury made a major impact on Jesus. People watched as others dropped money into the treasury, creating a loud noise, and all would know who gave it. The rich people's willingness to give so much impressed the common people. However, Jesus was not impressed by these rich people, for they had much more money elsewhere. This was not a sacrifice for them, but an effort to draw praise from others. Jesus was amazed by the poor widow who gave two copper coins, which was all she had. To give out of abundance creates no pain, but the money of the widow created a painful question: what would she eat the next day? She gave her money not for praise of others but because of her faith in God and her devotion to him. Her giving took all she had.

The world today, in some ways, is much like the world in the time when Jesus walked the paths of Judea. Today, some people are very rich, with assets valued at over one billion dollars. In Jesus's world, there were rich people as well. How they obtained that wealth, I do not know. Perhaps some of them received it from an inheritance. Maybe some gained riches in the trade business from one country to the next.

Another group of well-to-do people was those who were successful with skills, abilities, or knowledge that the people needed. Today, there are physicians, lawyers, professors, people who own their own businesses, professional athletes, and the list goes on. In the world of Jesus, carpenters made the furniture that most people needed. Contractors built the temples, libraries, and government buildings. Teachers, writers, and philosophers contributed to the intellectual side of society.

At another level, there are people just getting by. In our society, these are the lower income people. They work in construction, agriculture, and restaurants, and some are day laborers. They do not have the knowledge and intellectual skills to move up the economic ladder. In Jesus's time, this group also existed. Day laborers were common. There were workers in the fields, shepherds who cared for livestock, and others who had limited abilities.

The last group is the poor. They have hardly any money. Many of these poor dwell in tents, or under bridges, or in facilities made for them and financed by churches, mission groups, and civic organizations. Many of them are veterans who sustained mental and/ or physical damage while in the military. Some are handicapped, some cannot read, some cannot speak English, some are illegal in this country, making finding a job difficult. There are many reasons why others cannot get a job or keep a job. In Jesus's time, many of the poor were sick, some had handicaps, some had no skills or talents, and some were widows. Their husbands who made the money for the family were gone.

Jesus made the statement, "This widow has put in more than all those who were contributing to the treasury." She had given all that she had. The difference was that she gave from her heart to her God and to others in need.

It is true that Jesus loves all people, and especially the poor. Remember Luke 6:20b (RSV): "Blessed are you poor, for yours is the kingdom of God." In Luke 18:22b (RSV), a rich young ruler asks Jesus what he should do to inherit eternal life. Jesus tells him, "Sell all that you have and distribute to the poor, and you will have treasure in heaven; and come, follow me." In addition, remember Luke 6:30a (RSV) where Jesus said, "Give to everyone who begs from you."

Jesus saw the heart of that woman. She was completely devoted to God. Each one of us should embrace that lesson.

SAYING 40

"Take, this is my body."
—Mark 14:22b (RSV)

"This is my blood of the covenant,
which is poured out for many."
—Mark 14:24b (RSV)

MOST CHURCHGOING PEOPLE recognize these words as they celebrate the Lord's Supper, Holy Communion, the Eucharist, or the Last Supper. This meal of wine, or fruit of the vine, and bread represent the body and blood of Jesus as stated above. Matthew, in his account of this meal, says that it is offered "for the forgiveness of sins" (Matthew 26:28 RSV). Thus, it is through Jesus Christ that sins are forgiven. Apostle Paul, in his writings, stated it another way: "Christ Jesus came into the world to save sinners" (Timothy 1:15b RSV).

However, most Christian churches unite in the celebration of communion. The churches may observe communion in somewhat different ways. Some use wine, some use grape juice, some use grapes, and others use different beverages. However, churches are different and do things in different ways. Many churches use different hymns. Many churches have worship on different days of the week. Many churches recite different prayers. Many churches use different musical instruments, and some churches use no instruments at all.

However, the union of thousands of churches comes about by celebrating the Lord's Supper and eating and drinking that sacred meal. This meal celebrates Christ's sacrifice of his life for us so that we can have forgiveness, salvation, and life eternal.

Years ago while I was a pastor in northern Ohio, I was also a campus minister at Kent State University. I would meet with my students and have worship once a week and, if necessary, more often. I was a Baptist minister, but my students were from various church affiliations. In one of our meetings, we were discussing the Lord's Supper and what it meant. One girl in the group did not identify with any denomination but did have common faith with everyone else. She said, "I go to different churches on Sunday and enjoy their different ways, but when I sense the need for the Lord's Supper, I then go directly to the Catholic Church. Their communion truly touches me spiritually." I believe she was doing the right thing as Christ led her. Communion pulls us together into a common faith. This common faith is a faith of believing in Christ, a faith of sharing his grace, and a faith of commitment to him as our Lord and Savior.

SAYING 41

"Man shall not live by bread alone."
—Luke 4:4 (RSV)

THIS SAYING IS found in two passages:

"Man shall not live by bread alone." (Luke4:4 RSV)

"Man shall not live by bread alone, but by every word that proceeds from the mouth of God." (Matthew 4:4 RSV)

Did Matthew and Luke have different understandings of what Jesus meant when he said, "Man shall not live by bread alone"? Perhaps they did.

Matthew was writing his gospel of Jesus for the Jews. He felt the need to quote Jesus's words exactly because Jesus quoted directly from Deuteronomy 8:3 (RSV), which says "that man does not live by bread alone, but that man lives by everything that proceeds from the mouth of the Lord." Matthew's mind seemed to be more on the latter part of Jesus's statement than the former part. What Matthew seems to be saying is that Jesus spoke of bread but meant the words of God. The words of God are what gives us life, as God intended. I do not believe God ever intended for humans to live outside the words, the purpose, and the meaning of God. Surely, God's intention was for humans to live in harmony with God. However, in the creative event God gave humans the freedom to choose being in harmony with God or to reject that harmony. The results of this freedom were sin, hate, greed, selfishness, lies, and many other consequences. Matthew says that true life is in the presence of God.

What then is Luke saying? Luke says, "Man shall not live by bread alone." That is all Luke gives us. What does he mean? Jesus was hungry and the tempter gave him a solution to his need. However, one meal does not provide a solution to hunger. Hunger can return later, and probably will return. Luke focuses on the meal. Food is important and it is a product of God's creation. Food helps us to live from day to day. But there are more things in life that give life meaning, such as grace, peace, forgiveness, hope, kindness, patience, and the presence of God.

Who was correct, Matthew or Luke? They both were. Luke says was that food is not the answer to a meaningful life, but it is essential for life. Matthew says that true life, which is more than existence, comes from the words and presence of God. As Jesus said in John 10:10b (NRSV), "I have come that they may have life and have it more abundantly."

SAYING 42

"Be silent and come out of him."
—Luke 4:35b (NRSV)

TO ME, THIS story shows the compassion of Jesus. Jesus was in the synagogue in Capernaum on the Sabbath. He was there to teach the people the truths of God and how to live according to those truths. On that day, a man was in the audience who had an unclean spirit or, as some would say, a severe mental illness. This man interrupted Jesus, calling him the Holy One of God. However, he shouted in a loud voice, "What have you to do with us?" Apparently, he felt that Jesus's teachings had no relevance to him nor his condition. Not only was he a sick man, but he also had fits that were most visible to the people present. Jesus immediately responded to the man in need by removing his sickness and his fits. The people present were amazed at what Jesus had done.

In this story, Jesus showed compassion when he stopped his teaching to deal with an individual in need. When I was a young person, I thought Jesus had too much to do to take time to listen to me. I was wrong. Jesus is never too busy to touch the lives of those in need. He always has time to listen to our prayers, to hear our frustrations and hurts, to speak to our needs, and to comfort us in time of grief.

When we follow the example of Jesus and show compassion by helping the homeless, by comforting the sick, by visiting the lonely, or by caring for the unloved, we will be truly blessed. For there is no greater blessing than the happiness we feel when we do the will of God.

SAYING 43

"I must preach the good news of the
kingdom of God to the other cities also;
for I was sent for this purpose."
—Luke 4:43b (RSV)

"The Spirit of the Lord is upon me, because he has
anointed me to preach good news to the poor."
—Luke 4: 18a (RSV)

I HAVE BASED this article on both verses in the book of Luke. In Luke 4:18, Jesus quotes a passage from the book of Isaiah.

> The spirit of the Lord God is upon me, because the Lord has anointed me; he has sent me to bring good news to oppressed. (Isaiah 61:1a NRSV)

In reading this verse Jesus identifies himself with Isaiah's task to preach the good news to the poor people. In Luke 4:43, Jesus again states his purpose of preaching the good news. Therefore, based on the words of Jesus, the most important thing for him to do was to preach the gospel.

Usually in the ancient world of Israel, like many other locations throughout the world, when a list of names, actions, or tasks is stated, the most important is mentioned first and the rest of the list is in descending order of importance. For example, Mark 3:13–19 states that Jesus called to himself twelve disciples: Simon (Peter), James, John, Andrew, Philip, Bartholomew, Matthew, Thomas, James, Thaddeus, Simon, and Judas. Jesus called Peter first, and Peter became the leader of the disciples. Matthew 10:2–4 also mentions Peter first, but mentions Andrew second (a bit of a change from the first passage), followed by James and John. In Exodus 20:1–17, the Ten Commandments are listed in order as God voiced them, with the first commandment being, "You shall have no other gods before me." That is the foremost commandment of the ten.

This is true to a large degree in our world today. In our country, as in many other locations throughout the world, the first-born child of a family is indeed the most important child. This is a greater truth if the firstborn is a son. These first-born sons many times end up with the same name as their father.

Jesus gives us a list from the book of Isaiah 61:1–3, as recorded in Luke 4:18–19.

> The Spirit of the Lord God is upon me, because the Lord has anointed me to bring good tidings to the afflicted; he has sent me to bind up the broken hearted, to proclaim liberty to the captives, and opening the prison to those who are bound; to proclaim the year of the Lord's favor." (Isaiah 61:1–2 RSV)

> "The Spirit of the Lord is upon me, because he has anointed me to preach the good news to the poor. He has sent me to proclaim release to the captives and recovering of sight to the blind, to set at liberty those who are oppressed, to proclaim the acceptable year of the Lord." (Luke 4:18–19 RSV)

God gave this list of tasks to the Old Testament prophet. Jesus affirms those tasks for himself with the first in importance being "to preach good news to the poor." That is what Jesus did, along with other important tasks, because it was first in importance. We see the importance of preaching mentioned again in Luke 4:43: "I must preach the good news of the kingdom of God to the other cities also; for I was sent for this purpose."

That concept should be of primary importance in today's churches. Is that the most important task in most of our churches? I believe it is not. That task is accomplished through continuous study, prayer, and preparation. In 1970, James D. Smart wrote a book titled *The Strange Silence of the Bible in the Church*. Smart wrote that the Bible was of little use in many churches.[11] That was over fifty years ago. Where are we today? Preaching comes from the Bible. Preaching is to discover God's message and deliver it to the people. Jesus said that preaching was his primary task. Thus, preaching should be of primary importance in today's churches.

---

[11] James D. Smart, *The Strange Silence of the Bible in the Church: A Study in Hermeneutics* (Philadelphia: Westminster Press, 1970).

SAYING 44

"Man, your sins are forgiven you."
—Luke 5:20 (RSV)

I BELIEVE THIS section of scripture should be titled "The Religious Leaders Who Missed the Joy of God."

This story is about a paralyzed man who was lowered through the roof of a building by his friends in order to be before Jesus. He was hoping Jesus would heal him of his illness. Jesus said to the man, "Man, your sins are forgiven you." Immediately, the Pharisees began to react. They said that Jesus spoke blasphemies and that he could not forgive sins. Jesus told the paralyzed man to rise, take his bed, and go home. The Scriptures tell us that he rose, got his bed, and went home glorifying God. What a joyful occasion that must have been. The crowd of people also glorified God for what they had seen. This was truly a time of joy and thanksgiving. However, the religious leaders missed the joy of the moment.

These religious leaders were so concerned with criticizing Jesus, ridiculing Jesus, and speaking their disbelief in Jesus that they missed the joy of the moment. How happy everyone should have been by a paralyzed man getting to walk again. However, the religious leaders did not care about the man who was healed.

In our world today, many people are so full of hate, bitterness, anger, deceit, greed, and envy that they miss the beauty and joy of life. They miss the joy of children at play, the wind blowing through the trees, the smile of a young girl, the beauty of a sunset, and the sounds of birds chirping in the early morning. They miss the reunion of a soldier coming home, the excitement of young people graduating from school, and the beauty of the snow on a winter day. They miss the friendship of a dear friend, the sound of the hymn "Amazing Grace," and the beauty of dogwood trees and azalea bushes in bloom in the early spring. They miss so much, and all of these are joys given to us by a loving God.

SAYING 45

"Blessed are you poor, for yours
is the kingdom of God."
—Luke 6:20b (RSV)

WHY DID MATTHEW write that Jesus said, "Blessed are the poor in spirit," but Luke wrote that Jesus said, "Blessed are you poor"? The answer seems to be that Jesus preached and taught throughout the holy lands in different towns, on different mountains, and on different plains, to different people at different times. I am sure Jesus preached numerous times on the theme of blessings. Matthew 5:1 records that Jesus "went up on the mountain." In Luke 6:17, Jesus "stood on a level place." In Matthew 4:24–25 the author lists the towns and areas from whence the people came to hear Jesus preach and heal: Galilee, Decapolis, Jerusalem, Judea, and beyond the Jordan. In Luke 6:17, the author lists the towns and areas as Judea, Jerusalem, Tyre, and Sidon. Therefore, Jesus spoke on blessings in two different locations at two different times; Matthew recorded one of those events and Luke recorded a different event.

Why did Luke write more about the poor than Matthew did? From my perspective, Matthew was more interested in the sayings of Jesus. Luke, on the other hand, was referred to as "the beloved physician" by Paul. As a physician, he was more concerned about pain, hurt, hunger, sorrow, and rejection. Luke's concerns relate more directly to the poor, and Luke brought them to the forefront of his writings.

A few examples of this fact are as follows. In Luke 4:18a (RSV), the author quotes Isaiah 61:1, stating, "The Spirit of the Lord is upon me, because he has anointed me to preach good news to the poor." In Luke 7:22 (RSV), Luke writes, "Go and tell John what you have seen and heard: the blind receive their sight, the lame walk, the lepers are cleansed, and the deaf hear, the dead are raised up, the poor have good news preached to them." In Luke 14:21b (RSV), Jesus says, "Go out quickly to the streets and lanes of the city, and bring in the poor and maimed and blind and lame." The clearest statement of Jesus about the poor is in Luke 6:30a (NIV): "Give to everyone who begs from you."

Jesus's had concern for the poor is beyond debate. It should be continued in today's world through the lives of those who profess him as Lord.

SAYING 46

"Your sins are forgiven."
—Luke 7:48b (RSV)

THIS INCIDENT OF Jesus saying, "Your sins are forgiven" reminds us that Jesus said the same words to the paralytic who was lowered through the roof in Luke 5:20. As in the story of the paralytic, Jesus is rejected by the religious leaders, who say, "This man is blaspheming." Jesus responds by saying, "Why do you think evil in your hearts?" Jesus then tells the paralytic, "Rise, take up your bed, and go home." Why do so many people immediately think of the bad, the wrong, and the evil?

Again, Jesus uses the words, "Your sins are forgiven," as recorded in Luke 7:48. Here, a woman appears at an all-men's party or gathering. The Bible does not tell us much about this woman, but the Bible does say that she was a sinful person. What that means, we cannot be sure. She probably made her living by entertaining men. The men she might have entertained had no love for her, no concern for her, but just wanted to use her.

In this story, the picture is somewhat different in that the person in need is not a paralytic man but a sinful woman. The paralytic went down through the roof to see Jesus. The sinful woman went down on her knees to kiss Jesus's feet. The paralytic needed the healing of his body. The woman needed forgiveness for her sinful life. In both cases, Jesus was ridiculed for the good that he did.

We cannot heal a person's body, although physicians can help with healing. We cannot forgive people their sins. What then can we do? We can pray to a gracious Lord for healing of the body to take place. God hears us and then it is in his hands. We can love the sinner and lead him or her to Jesus. These two stories tell us what God expects us to do. We can and should pray for healing of those in need. We can and should love the sinner and point him or her to Jesus. Therefore, our prayer should be, "Lord use us, Lord use us."

SAYING 47

"Blessed rather are those who hear
the word of God and obey it."
—Luke 11:28b (RSV)

JESUS WAS IN a town and a crowd gathered about him. By this time in his life, he was well known by many people because of his healing of sick people, his teaching and preaching which touched many lives, and his love for children and adults as well.

In this crowd a woman called out, "Blessed is the woman who gave you birth and nursed you." To this Jesus replied, "Blessed rather are those who hear the word of God and obey it." Why did Jesus answer in that fashion?

Jesus did not reject her words. In fact, Mary was blessed to have a son named Jesus who did so much good for the people and taught them of the love and forgiveness of the heavenly father. However, Jesus knew of his coming death, and said, "The Son of man is to be delivered into the hands of men" (Luke 9:44 RSV). Jesus knew what his mother would endure when he was tried and nailed to the cross, and experienced his horrible death.

No mother should have to endure that. What Jesus was saying is that a greater blessing for anyone is to hear the word of God and obey it. By "obeying it," he meant to believe it, to live it, and to share it with others. That is what I would call an everlasting blessing. Thus, God will neither leave us nor forsake us, if we hear the word and keep it.

SAYING 48

"Woman, you are freed from your infirmity."
—Luke 13:12b (RSV)

JESUS SAYS THIS to the stooped woman. She had been bent over for eighteen years. Jesus was teaching in a Jewish synagogue when he noticed her infirmity. He called her to himself, laid his hands on her, and said to her, "Woman, you are freed from your infirmity." What a wonderful day it was for that woman. What a wonderful day it was for Jesus, for he loved to do good for people: women, men, or children. What a wonderful day it was for a number of people to watch Jesus change a person's life. However, the ruler of the synagogue opposed it. He missed the joy and the blessing of the moment.

Many people love to see others doing good deeds. I have seen on television where a group of people supplied food and water when there was a tornado, a hurricane, a flood, or a fire that destroyed homes. What a joy to see that. It means some people care.

Several days ago, my wife and I were in Paducah, Kentucky. We were driving through a Walmart parking lot when we saw this woman with her sign on the edge of the street. We decided to go into Walmart, purchase what we needed, and then return to the car. After that, we would visit her and give her money, which she probably needed. When we returned to the car, we noticed she was gone. Our failure brought on sorrow to each one of us. Why did it bother us? Because God gave us a chance to help someone in need. We failed to do it. God gave us a lesson. When you see the need, do not delay. The opportunity might pass you by.

SAYING 49

He who is faithful in a very little is faithful
also in much; and he who is dishonest in
a very little is dishonest also in much.

—Luke 16:10 (RSV)

Train up a child in the way he should go,
and when he is old he will not depart from it.

—Proverbs 22:6 (RSV)

CHAPTER 16 OF Luke's gospel is somewhat different from the rest of the chapters because it begins and ends with a parable. Between these two parables is a collection of wisdom sayings, or sermon summaries, much like we find in Matthew's Sermon on the Mount (Matthew 5:1–7:27) and Luke's Sermon on the Plain (Luke 6:17–49). In fact, Luke 16:10–18 is very reminiscent of the wisdom sayings of the Old Testament. Take for example Proverbs 22:6, which states, "Train up a child in the way he should go, and when he is old he will not depart from it."

The question I have concerning Luke 16:10 is when would a person learn to be faithful in little things and how was that done? Thus, I reflect on Proverbs 22:6. Such learning would have to come about while that person was a child. In that case, we can see Luke 16:10 as a very important lesson for young couples who are raising children.

This world is a new experience for young children; they notice most everything their parents do or say. They see when their parents are kind to other people. They see if their parents are rude to others. Most all that they see or hear are new experiences, which they will carry within themselves the rest of their life on earth.

What their parents say or do becomes a lesson for them and gives them the lesson that life should be lived in this manner. What kind of people do we want our children to become? The old adage "like father, like son" carries a good amount of truth.

When the child sees the parents give money to the poor, the child learns that poor people are important and they need to be aided. When the child sees his or her parents give food and water to the destitute, the child learns that needy people need help. When the child sees his or her parents help the neighbor next door, the child learns that all of us need help occasionally. When the child sees the parents going to church and taking the children to church, the child learns that there is a God, and that God loves them.

There are many, many more lessons—positive lessons—children can and do learn from caring and loving parents. What the child learns as a young person will go with that person the rest of his or her life.

SAYING 50

"Truly, I say to you, today you will
be with me in Paradise."

—Luke 23:43b (RSV)

THIS IS A great saying, or quotation, to close out this book. Jesus says this while on the cross. Two other men were crucified alongside Jesus. One of the men asked Jesus, "Are you not the Christ? Save yourself and us" (Luke 23:39b RSV). He was not concerned about Jesus but about himself and ending his own suffering.

The second man recognized Jesus as divine and said, "Jesus, remember me when you come into your kingdom" (Luke 23:42b RSV). To that statement Jesus replied, "Truly, I say to you, today you will be with me in Paradise," promising the second man that after death they would be together in Paradise.

What then is Paradise? Many Christian writers tell us that the word *paradise* is an old Persian word that meant garden or park. The Persian word in time passed into many different languages, but continued to mean garden or park. Therefore, what Jesus said to the second man was that the two of them after death would end up together in a garden or, as Revelation 2:7 reads, in the "garden of God."

How do biblical scholars today define paradise? Some individuals define paradise as heaven. Another group of scholars holds that paradise is an intermediate place for believers waiting for the resurrection. Many individuals hold views different from these two groups. As for my position, I believe that shortly after death, I will be with Jesus—and being with him is heaven enough for me.

As Christians, our God-given task is far more important than debating an issue. That task is to lead people to an understanding of Jesus and a belief in Jesus as the Son of God. Through Jesus, they can have a life of meaning, a life of purpose, a life of internal peace, and a life of contentment. That life is also everlasting.

WHY WRITE ABOUT MEMORABLE SAYINGS?

Why did I write about memorable sayings, or quotations, or one-liners? That comes out of my background. When I was in high school, our school library received *The Louisville Courier Journal* newspaper daily. The thing that interested me most was the quotable quotations, or what I call memorable sayings. When a news item in the *Journal* did not completely fill a column in the paper, the editors would fill the space with quotable sayings from notable people such as Benjamin Franklin, Charles Dickens, and Albert Einstein. I became fascinated with what meaning a few words could convey. Through that experience in high school, I have forever been enthralled with quotable sayings.

Over the years in reading the scriptures, I came to understand that Matthew, the disciple of Jesus, also became fascinated with quotable sayings of Jesus. That is the basis for my writing the memorable sayings. When Jesus spoke a memorable saying, he was saying something of great value.

SOME OF MY FAVORITE SAYINGS

Socrates (469–389 BC, Greek philosopher)
> There is no possession more valuable than a good and faithful friend.

> By all means marry. If you get a good wife, you will be happy. If you get a bad one, you will become a philosopher.

Plato (427–347 BC, Greek philosopher)
> Man—a being in search of meaning.

> There is no harm in repeating a good thing.

Aristotle (384–322 BC, Greek philosopher)
> Happiness depends upon ourselves.

> Good habits formed at youth make all the difference.

Alexander the Great (356–323 BC, Macedonian king)
> I would rather live a short life of glory than a long one of obscurity.

Marcus Aurelius (AD 121–180, Roman emperor and Stoic philosopher)
The whole universe is change and life itself is but what you deem it. (*Meditations,* Book 4, Section 3)

A man's true delight is to do the things he was made for.

Waste no more time arguing what a good man should be. Be one. (*Meditations* Book 10, Section 16)

Julius Caesar (100–44 BC, Roman emperor)
I came, I saw, I conquered.

The die is cast.

William Shakespeare (AD 1564–1616, English playwright and poet)
"Men at some time are masters of their fates. (*Julius Caesar* 1.2.139)

Benjamin Franklin (AD 1706–1790, writer and statesman)
Haste makes waste. (*Poor Richard's Almanack* 1753)

Thomas Jefferson (AD 1743–1826, third President of the United States)
Never spend your money before you have it. (1811 letter to Cornelia Jefferson Randolph)

Charles Dickens (AD 1812–1870, English author)
It was the best of times, it was the worst of times. (*A Tale of Two Cities*)

Anne Frank (AD 1929–1945, Jewish author)
Whoever is happy will make others happy. (*The Diary of a Young Girl*)

Unknown Author
When the angels speak, write it down.

Printed in the United States
by Baker & Taylor Publisher Services